Neo-Existentialism

Neo-Existentialism

How to Conceive of the Human Mind
after Naturalism's Failure

Markus Gabriel

Edited by

Jocelyn Maclure

With contributions by

Jocelyn Benoist, Andrea Kern, and
Charles Taylor

polity

First published in 2018 by Polity Press

Polity Press
65 Bridge Street
Cambridge CB2 1UR, UK

Polity Press
101 Station Landing
Suite 300
Medford, MA 02155, USA

ISBN-13: 978-1-5095-3247-6
ISBN-13: 978-1-5095-3248-3 (pb)

A catalogue record for this book is available from the British Library.

Typeset in 10.5 on 12 pt Sabon
by Fakenham Prepress Solutions, Fakenham, Norfolk NR21 8NN
Printed and bound in Great Britain, by Clays Ltd

The publisher has used its best endeavours to ensure that the URLs for external websites referred to in this book are correct and active at the time of going to press. However, the publisher has no responsibility for the websites and can make no guarantee that a site will remain live or that the content is or will remain appropriate.

Every effort has been made to trace all copyright holders, but if any have been inadvertently overlooked the publisher will be pleased to include any necessary credits in any subsequent reprint or edition.

For further information on Polity, visit our website:

politybooks.com

Contents

Introduction

Reasonable Naturalism and the Humanistic Resistance to Reductionism[1]

Jocelyn Maclure

Markus Gabriel is one of the most exciting minds among the new generation of academic philosophers. He defends bold views on large metaphysical questions. In his previous work, he argued that the abuse of constructivism in ontology and epistemology called for a renewed kind of realism centered on the plurality of domains of objects or "fields of sense" that make up our reality. His work is based on an impressive command of a variety of past and present philosophical traditions. There is no sharp divide, for him, between philosophy and its history. And, as he points out in the opening chapter of this volume, he views the continental/analytic distinction as nonsensical and debilitating.

Gabriel adds his voice to a distinguished tradition of humanistic scholars who worry about the overreach of scientific discourse in our understanding of human reality and experience. A strand of that tradition finds its root in German philosophy, as exemplified by the responses gathered in this volume. This is not something that was planned in the design of this book when I reached out to a number of potential commentators, but it turned out that Charles Taylor, Jocelyn Benoist and Andrea Kern all implicitly or explicitly draw upon traditions such as idealism and phenomenology to support Gabriel's take-down of naturalism in analytic philosophy of mind. Charles Taylor is a long-time critic of scientism and reductive naturalism.[2] Jocelyn Benoist is a leading expert on the origins of phenomenology and on the links between phenomenology and analytic philosophy.[3] In her work in metaphysics and epistemology, Andrea Kern is articulating a brand of neo-Aristotelianism influenced by Kant and German idealism. All three, like Gabriel, have decidedly moved beyond the analytic/continental divide in contemporary Western philosophy.

In the piece which is the cornerstone of this volume, Gabriel challenges the hegemony of naturalism in analytic philosophy of mind. He starts from the classic problem of how the mind fits in the natural world. How can physical and biological processes which are not, as far as we can tell, conscious give rise to mental states such as desires, beliefs, and intentions? Once we give up, on the basis of our best natural sciences, the belief in an immaterial soul, how do we explain our conscious subjective experience and how does it map onto everything that we know about the physical world? Given that Cartesian "substance dualism" is no longer an option, the obvious temptation is to reduce the mental to more basic natural properties, such as brain processes, which are themselves explainable in terms of physical laws, mechanisms, and properties. But since it is not clear how studying various regions of the brain and neural activity is supposed to reveal what is a subjective experience, such as experiencing a first kiss with someone on whom you have a crush, many wonder whether we are confronted with a "hard problem" that may never be solved by the natural sciences, the neurosciences included.[4]

Gabriel associates naturalism, among other things, with the choice to see the mind as a natural kind and to reduce it to physical mechanisms. He thinks this choice is misguided. He wants to "put pressure on the entire framework" which made of naturalism an overarching speculative metaphysics rather than a sound approach to the study of the natural world. In contrast, he sketches a position that he calls "Neo-Existentialism," which is:

the view that there is no single phenomenon or reality corresponding to the ultimately very messy umbrella term "the
mind." ... what unifies the various phenomena subsumed
under the messy concept of "the mind" after all is that they
are all consequences of the attempt of the human being to
distinguish itself both from the purely physical universe and
from the rest of the animal kingdom. In so doing, our self-
portrait as specifically minded creatures evolved in light of
our equally varying accounts of what it is for non-human
beings to exist. (pp. 9–10)

We may wonder, as Taylor does in his commentary, whether
the reference to existentialism is the best way to characterize
the view that he is putting forward and to bring together the
philosophers from whom he is drawing inspiration. Gabriel's
"Neo-Existentialism" is much broader than the philosophical
views expounded by Sartre and de Beauvoir after the Second
World War. Some of the preeminent early figures of the
movement such as Merleau-Ponty and Camus later explicitly
rejected the label. Neo-Existentialism appears to include
elements drawn from what is sometimes called philosophies
of consciousness or subjectivity, German idealism, phenomenology, hermeneutics (as applied to selfhood, or narrative
theories of the self) and philosophies of existence.

Gabriel clearly sides with those who reject the identity
theory between the brain and the mind, as well as with those
who think that the mind is not only in the head. I see him
as a philosophical anthropologist who draws our attention
to the inescapably cultural or social dimension of the mind.
The mind is the result not only of the neural activity which
makes consciousness possible but also of the self-interpreting,
meaning-making, and collective symbolic activity which is
the trademark of our species. As Gabriel puts it, "We should
not expect that all phenomena which have been described
from the intentional stance over the millennia, and for
which we have some kind of record of documenting an
inner life, could possibly be theoretically unified by finding
an equivalent natural substratum for them" (p. 41). The
German concept of "*Geist*" better captures the permeability
between nature and culture than the English "mind." One
could perhaps say that *Geist* encompasses both biological
and cultural evolution.[5]

That being said, Gabriel's Neo-Existentialism appears to be ambiguous with regard to the exact way to think about the brain–mind relationship. On the one hand, he clearly states that he does not want his view to deny what has been firmly established by the natural sciences. He thereby accepts that having a certain kind of brain is a necessary condition for having a mind. He does not challenge the fact that all mental events have brain correlates. On the other hand, he asserts that "The notion that mind has to fit into the natural order is nothing but the most recent mythology, the most recent attempt to fit all phenomena that are relevant to human action explanation into an all-encompassing structure" (p. 38).

I wholeheartedly agree with Gabriel that we have good reasons to reject the physicalist monistic claim according to which mental states are only or primordially physical states. But one might think at this point that, broadly speaking, "naturalist" philosophers of mind and neuroscientists could more modestly claim that there are physical requisites for something like the intentional stance to be possible. Brain states are at least partly constitutive of mental states; they necessarily show up in any plausible causal story about the occurrence of mental events. This does not logically commit one to the view that mental states can be reduced to brain states or that they are epiphenomenal. Gabriel could perhaps recognize more empathically that to try to figure out what needed to happen in our neurobiological evolution for something like subjective experience to occur, or what needs to happen in my brain for me to enjoy a macchiato, is a scientific endeavor of tremendous importance. Once we recognize, as Gabriel does, that having a certain kind of brain is a necessary condition for having a mind, there will be a naturalist element in our theory. In his chapter, Gabriel seems to oscillate between including scientific naturalism within a richer philosophical view and a wholesale rejection of naturalism. I am myself inclined to think that, given the extraordinary explanatory power of the natural sciences, what we might call "reasonable naturalism" should be worked into a broader philosophical view of reality.

In fact, there is a way to read Gabriel's chapter that suggests that *reductionism*, rather than *naturalism*, is the real target of his critique. Naturalists do think that the mind "fits" in the "natural order," but they do not have to hold a monistic ontology according to which everything that exists must be reducible to a natural kind or that the progress of science will lead to the gradual elimination of all mentalistic concepts. For instance, many accept that one cannot explain social facts and institutions without invoking the causal efficacy of collective intentionality.[6]

If I am on the right track, further developing and specifying Neo-Existentialism will necessarily require a more direct and sustained engagement with some of the, to my mind, more plausible options in analytic philosophy of mind. I am thinking here of more or less overlapping positions such as "non-reductive physicalism," "property dualism," and "emergentism." Spelling out why Neo-Existentialists are dissatisfied with these positions will help those, like me, who cannot endorse standard reductionist physicalism but who are as yet unsure about what is the best available theory.

In any case, I submit that Gabriel could accept what might be called the "underdetermination thesis": the descriptions offered by the natural sciences cannot saturate our understanding of the mental and, *eo ipso*, of ourselves as human agents. If it is true that conceptions of the mind that contradict the laws of physics or of evolutionary biology should be seen as false, there are nonetheless a number of ways in which we can understand the mind that are incompatible between themselves and yet compatible with the laws of nature. Theories which argue, for instance, that the mind is *both* natural and cultural/intersubjective can agree that there are indeed neural preconditions for subjective experience, while still maintaining, like the authors gathered in this volume, that the mind is more than the brain and that naturalistic reductionism will never be able fully to explain mindedness. Leaving aside the sci-fi thought experiments that enjoy disproportionate popularity in analytic philosophy of mind, having a body and being embedded in a lifeworld or culture are, as far as we can tell, *also* partly constitutive of mental life.

As Gabriel, Taylor, Benoist, and Kern point out in their own way, mental states can be modified by other mental states, whereas natural facts are generally mind-independent:

my false belief that a normal DNA sequence is made of six nucleotide bases does not change the fact that it is made of four. But my belief that the pill that I am taking following the researcher's orders is a therapeutic drug and not a placebo might very well change my subjective state with regard to my symptoms even if it is in fact a placebo.

Or, to take another example: the tension that I feel in my hamstring when I push hard at the end of a marathon can very well be interpreted as utterly normal in that context, but as more painful and worrisome when I feel a similar sensation as I am quietly walking towards the subway station. What is going on in my muscle fibre, nervous system, and associated brain region is independent of my beliefs, but my conscious experience – how the tension feels to me – cannot be reduced to these physical properties. This seems to bring us close to "property dualism" – i.e., the position according to which physical properties do not exhaust the explanation of a mental phenomenon at the ontological level.[7] Property dualism need not revert back to Cartesian substance dualism, as mental states can be seen as made of not particularly mysterious physical *and* social properties. The property dualist, like Gabriel, can say that cycling supervenes on bicycles but cannot be reduced to it. Cycling also requires the presence of a set of social meanings and practices put in place by intentional agents. A reasonable naturalist should not want to deny that.

Just as contrasting Neo-Existentialism with non-reductive theories will help move the discussion further, readers will also wonder to what extent Gabriel agrees with heterodox philosophers of mind, neuroscientists, and cognitive scientists who see the mind as embodied, embedded, and extended. I leave aside here an examination of the differences and similarities between the externalist theories which all assert that the mind cannot only be located in the head. Among contemporary externalists, some suggest that the mind, or at least cognition, includes artifacts such as cognitive tools,[8] whereas others argue that the relationships between mind, body, and world are so intricate that the boundaries between them ought to be seen as thoroughly porous.[9]

I wrote above that Gabriel's Neo-Existentialism appears much broader than historical existentialism. That said, one of the points in common between Neo-Existentialism and French atheistic existentialism is that, just as, say, Sartre's "L'existentialisme est un humanisme" was for many, after the bleak and tormented years of the Second World War, a much awaited world-view, the kind of humanistic-yet-realist view sketched out by Gabriel in his work is much needed in a context where reductive naturalism, posthumanism, and the remnants of postmodernism remain, to different degrees, culturally influential. Many philosophers of mind, neuroscientists, and cognitive scientists will want to question specific arguments made by Gabriel and the commentators and deplore some of their omissions. This is fair, as this is how Neo-Existentialism can become more robust. But for those of us who feel ill at ease with the hegemony of reductive naturalism in some influential quarters of academia and of the broader culture, these views will be seen as evidence that the resistance is coming.

1

Neo-Existentialism: How to Conceive of the Human Mind after Naturalism's Failure[1]

Markus Gabriel

It is a widespread assumption in contemporary scientific culture that the existence of mental objects rests on very shaky ground. By contrast, physical objects are supposed to exist beyond any reasonable doubt. Let us call this *the post-Cartesian ontological asymmetry*. Whereas Descartes, like many of his predecessors, unabashedly argued for the inverse asymmetry, claiming not only that the mind is better known (to the mind) than any other object but that it also enjoys a privileged mode of existence (being closer in ontological kind to God than to material substance), the order of the ontological universe has subsequently been reversed. Be that as it may, what would entitle *us* to continue to believe in ontological asymmetry? Are there any deeper reasons to privilege either physical or mental objects in the best account of what there is?

Very roughly, in our scientific age one might begin to give voice to one's post-Cartesian preferences by pointing out that, while there evidently are rocks, bacteria, paramecia, and fingernails, Faust, Macbeth, and the Fountain of Youth clearly do not exist, regardless of the fact that there are various discursive practices ("language-games") which entitle us to engage in a game of make-believe involving talk about these kinds of things. These kinds of things are typically called "fictional," where this means that they "are individuals first introduced in a work of fiction" (Brock and Everett 2015: 3).[2] They depend for their existence on minds in a way in which rocks do not. It borders on triviality that Macbeth would not have existed had there been no minds, and those who hold the view known as "fictional irrealism" deny that he exists at all, sometimes on the ground that, had he existed, he would have been a mere figment of imagination and in that sense nothing that could count as actually existing.[3]

In this context, it is tempting to group the mind itself with fictional objects to the extent to which one's reasons to grant the latter a reduced ontological status (if any) are tantamount to one's reasons for denying them mind-independence. If the mind were mind-dependent in the same way as the Fountain of Youth, in an ontological framework privileging mind-independence in our account of what there is, we would have reasons to downgrade the mind as a whole.

Arguably, at this point a typical representative of contemporary scientific culture will argue that the mind is not mind-dependent in the same way in which the Fountain of Youth is, as the mind can ultimately be identified with a physical object: the brain. Despite the complexities of figuring out how exactly to make sense of such an identity claim, given, among other things, the apparent epistemological asymmetry of mind and brain, the stereotypical modern scientist will hope that the impression that there is a real distinction at the level of the apparent epistemological asymmetry sooner or later goes away, as science makes progress with respect to the mind. The better we actually know the brain, the safer it will seem to identify mind and brain and to undermine our Cartesian "intuitions," our impression that the mind substantially differs from the brain.

In what follows, I will put pressure on the entire framework which gives rise to this branch of the modern scientific world-view. In particular, I will sketch a position I dub "Neo-Existentialism." Neo-Existentialism is the view that there is no single phenomenon or reality corresponding to the ultimately very messy umbrella term "the mind." Rather, the phenomena typically grouped together under this heading are located on a spectrum ranging from the obviously physical to the non-existing. However, what unifies the various phenomena subsumed under the messy concept of "the mind" after all is that they all are consequences of the attempt of the human being to distinguish itself both from the purely physical universe and from the rest of the animal kingdom. In so doing, our self-portrait as specifically minded creatures evolved in light of our equally varying accounts of what it is for non-human beings to exist.

The fundamental tenet of Neo-Existentialism is that there is no single entity in the world picked out by our diachronically and synchronically differentiated mentalistic vocabulary, nothing which is conscious, self-conscious, aware of itself, neurotic, a processor of qualitative states, vigilant, intelligent, etc. What unifies our mentalistic vocabulary is the capacity to produce further items on the list of accounts of what it is not merely to blend in with a world replete with inanimate objects governed by physical laws of nature, on the one hand, and animals driven by biological parameters, on the other.

Our self-portrait as minded is in place in order to help us make sense of the fact that we do not belong to the domain of what merely exists in an anonymous manner, as it were. We are neither exactly like rocks nor exactly like a beetle lying on a rock. Our conception of ourselves as minded was forged over millennia of history in which it was taken for granted that, whatever distinguishes us from the remainder of what there is, it can only be accounted for in mentalistic terms. This structure is the breeding ground of the very notion of human being, the notion without which we would be in no position to wonder what the relation between mind and non-mental nature could possibly be.

Over the course of known documented history, humanity has developed highly nuanced accounts of what distinguishes us from inanimate and animal nature. In my view, this is the real source behind what Huw Price has aptly called "the placement issue" (Price 2011: 187–8). To put this problem as bluntly as possible, it arises from wondering how the mind – i.e., the manifold objects, if any, picked out by our mentalistic vocabulary – fits into the purely natural order.[4]

My own term for "the purely natural order" is *the universe*. I distinguish between *the universe* and *the world*. Whereas the former refers to the domain of objects studied by our best natural sciences (maybe ideally by futuristic unified physics or, depending on the status of the unity/disunity of science, by any relevant ensemble of established present and future disciplines), the latter is the hypothetical all-encompassing domain of objects. For reasons spelled out elsewhere (Gabriel 2015a), I believe that this idea of the world should be reformulated: we should understand the world neither as an all-encompassing domain of objects nor as the all-encompassing domain of facts, but as what I call "the field of sense of all fields of sense." Here, a "field of sense" (FOS) is my name for a domain of objects individuated by what corresponds to the right way of thinking about its objects. The right way of thinking about the objects in a given domain is the way which lets us grasp them as they are under the descriptions which aptly characterize them as being whatever they are (ibid.).[5] The universe is an FOS within a domain encompassing further FOSs. It is nested within an open system of FOSs. There is no overall, all-encompassing FOS. I call this result from the ontology of FOSs the "no-world-view," and I summarize it in the expression that the world does not exist (Gabriel 2015b). According to Neo-Existentialism, the mind belongs neither to the natural order (the universe) nor to the world. However, it exists in a whole series of FOSs in such a way that the various phenomena grouped together under the umbrella term "the mind" do not pick out a clearly delineated object or range of objects. Nevertheless, there is an invariant unifying structure which holds our mentalistic vocabulary together. This structure is what I call "Geist." Given that Geist is a technical notion here designed to account for the invariant in the background of the messy variations of mentalistic vocabulary, it is guaranteed to be less messy than the series of mentalistic vocabularies we happen to find. Notice that according to my proposal some parts or subdomains of Geist are included in the universe. All that I will be arguing for is that neither all parts nor the whole of Geist can exist in the universe.

If the mind as the fusion of various objects brought into existence by Geist's historically shifting attempts to make sense of the distinction between human and non-human being exists at all, according to my background ontology it has to fit into some FOS or other. Even if the mind is a fictional object (or a nest of fictional objects), it will find its place in a suitable FOS distinguished from other FOSs. This will be true both *horizontally* – in comparison with other, say, literary or cinematic fictions – and *vertically* – in the context of FOSs belonging to an entirely different, specifically non-fictional category, such as the FOS of astrophysics. The right kind of ontological pluralism that allows for a plurality of domains related to each other in a larger order composed of different categorically distinct pockets easily accommodates the mind whatever its nature turns out to be. Ontological pluralism trivially leaves room for the mind, as many of the items picked out by various mentalistic vocabularies (consciousness, awareness, emotions, being awake, etc.) can be accommodated without having to place them in the same ontological realm (the same FOS) as baryonic matter, galaxies, or the cerebellum, say.

It is harder for the metaphysical monist to do justice to the respectable trains of thought that amount to a placement problem. In order to see why, imagine two extreme views, *brute materialism* and *brute idealism*. Brute materialism claims that the only thing there is is the universe and that the universe is identical with material-energetic reality. Brute idealism is the most radical denial of this monism, as it maintains that all there is is mental – i.e., either some mental content or a mind, where mind and the mental are categorically juxtaposed to the material-energetic. Brute idealism denies the existence of non-mental objects.

On both extremes of metaphysical monism, in principle no placement problem arises. Brute materialism has no room for a conception of the mind that would lead to a puzzle about its place in nature (identified with the universe in the sense of the entirety of the material-energetic), and brute idealism, in turn, has no room for a conception of a nature that would motivate a puzzle about its relation to the mind.

Despite the fact that there is a massive return of grand metaphysics in both the so-called analytic and the so-called continental traditions of philosophy, the issues discussed in the philosophy of mind call for independent conceptual treatment.[6] The main reason for this can already be guessed from the broad strokes of my introductory remarks. If the placement problem were merely a metaphysical issue that needs to go away, we could easily circumvent it in indefinitely many ways by working out a metaphysical system close enough either to metaphysical pluralism or to metaphysical monism. All we would need to avoid is the obviously untenable position of metaphysical dualism in the sense of a view that subscribes both to the unity of reality and to its having two big chunks – matter and mind – separated by some kind of gulf.

Notoriously, even Descartes, who is usually invoked as a prime representative of the shortcomings of metaphysical dualism, admits that there is a problem here. He oscillates between an actual metaphysical dualism (belief in two substances – i.e., two categorically distinct kinds of things) and metaphysical monism, as he sometimes writes that, strictly speaking, only God is a substance.[7] If there is only one reality, it is indeed puzzling what one could mean by the assertion that there are two kinds of things within that reality, matter and mind. What is the nature of that reality which accounts for the emergence of an extraordinary duality within itself? So-called *neutral monism*, which is the view (or family of views) that there is a third kind of thing underlying the differentiation into the two kinds of things earlier identified, owes us an account of the nature of the extraordinary third kind of thing which avoids unwelcome regresses or unwarranted blockers thereof.

In what follows, I will argue that the widespread use of the term "naturalism" has proven to be a mere fig leaf to cover up the embarrassing lack of a suitable metaphysical account which both preserves the existence of the mind and raises the problem of its integration into a wider domain containing not only minds and their contents but events such as the Big Bang, the inflation of the universe, digestion, and objects such as fingernails, gauge bosons, and so forth. Naturalism is at best a mongrel term mingling together various philosophical commitments designed to avoid addressing the underlying metaphysical and epistemological issues head-on.

Naturalism in my view basically boils down to an avoidance strategy. The reason for its existence and widespread acceptance among philosophers and scientists alike in many parts of the world is ideological. Roughly speaking, by an "ideology" here I am referring to any attempt to present something that is an historically contingent representation of the human mind (a case of *Geist*) as a natural fact of the matter about us humans.[8] That naturalism can be seen as an ideology has aptly, albeit overly polemically, been remarked on by the late Hilary Putnam in his *Philosophy in an Age of Science*:

> Today the most common use of the term "naturalism" might be described as follows: philosophers – perhaps even a majority of all the philosophers writing about issues in metaphysics, epistemology, philosophy of mind, and philosophy of language – announce in one or another conspicuous place in their essays and books that they are "naturalists" or that the view or account being defended is a "naturalist" one. This announcement, in its placing and emphasis, resembles the placing of the announcement in articles written in Stalin's Soviet Union that a view was in agreement with Comrade Stalin's; as in the case of the latter announcement, it is supposed to be clear that any view that is not "naturalist" (not in agreement with Comrade Stalin's view) is anathema and could not possibly be correct. A further very common feature is that, as a rule, "naturalism" is not *defined*. (Putnam 2012: 109ff.)

The comparison with Stalinism suggests a political background to the ideology of naturalism. With a pinch of salt and some irony, one could indeed make a case for the diagnosis that naturalism is Soviet historico-dialectical materialism without Soviets, history, and dialectics. It is a watered-down version of good old materialism. In this vein, it can be seen as an odd remainder of earlier stages of the Cold War – a simplified materialist ideology originally promoted by US-American ideological state apparatuses (including universities) in order to combat Soviet ideas. It would take at least a book-length discussion of the relation of the notion of ideology explicitly deployed here to the wider notion of (political) ideology to actually establish the details of such a sweeping claim. Suffice it to remind us of the fact that Marx and Engels back in their day introduced their brand of historical dialectical materialism with the human being at its center in order to combat the simplified materialist ideology which emerged together with positivism in their half of the nineteenth century.

Be that as it may, what is certainly correct in Putnam's diagnosis is that continued adherence to naturalism – whether on the level of scientific methodology or of substantial metaphysical commitment – is not simply a consequence of natural science. Generally, no overall world-view is recommended by any specific insight into the structure of the universe, understood as the domain under investigation by the natural sciences.[9]

One of the reasons for this is that, in order to arrive at any sufficient world-view with ambitions to completeness, we would have to give an account of which elements of human language and thought actually refer to something real. And no such account can easily be given without a good deal of philosophical work which divides fragments of human language and thought into different categories, such as the categories of referring and (non-referring) inferential vocabulary, say.[10] Which elements of thought latch onto an independent reality, a reality not consisting in binding thoughts internally together, cannot be settled by inspecting the universe.

This should be evident as long as we stick to the meaning of "the universe" as the domain of objects under investigation in the natural sciences and as long as logic is not included in the catalogue of our natural sciences. If it were, and if it, therefore, had a suitable domain of objects, naturalism would be false anyway, as independent reality would then encompass norms for thought as such – an ontological commitment unlikely to lend support to naturalism.

I Consciousness of the Gap

Contemporary scientists and philosophers alike regularly avow that the problem of consciousness is one of the last riddles we need to solve in order to finally sail into the safe haven of a fully naturalistic world-view. Here are two examples. First, the somewhat ironic opening line of Daniel Dennett's influential book *Consciousness Explained*: "Human consciousness is just about the last surviving mystery. A mystery is a phenomenon that people don't know how to think about – yet" (Dennett 1991: 21). Second, David

Chalmers opens his equally influential *The Conscious Mind* with a similar, albeit far from ironic confession:

> Consciousness is the biggest mystery. It may be the largest outstanding obstacle in our quest for a scientific understanding of the universe. ... Present-day scientific theories hardly touch the really difficult questions about consciousness. We do not just lack a detailed theory; we are entirely in the dark about how consciousness fits into the natural order. (Chalmers 1996: xi)

Minimally, the naturalistic world-view assumes that we ought to fit all phenomena into the natural order. Everything which dangles free from the natural order either does not really exist or is a surprising epiphenomenon and is, in any event, nothing which could interfere with the real. To claim that consciousness or the mind are mysteries or riddles is to claim that it is hard or maybe even impossible to figure out how consciousness or the mind can be part of nature in a scientifically respectable sense of "nature."

Here, the metaphysical assumption without which the mystery could not get off the ground is that "the natural order" cannot be maximal in the sense of including all phenomena. For, if "the natural order" were simply everything there is, it would be easy to see how consciousness "fits into the natural order." Naturalism had better not assume from the outset that consciousness does not exist or that no term in our mentalistic vocabulary is in the business of referring to something real. In order for there to be a mystery of any kind, the natural order has to be thought of in such a way that consciousness is not immediately accessible from within the natural order as we know it to be. That is to say, the naturalist has to restrict the meaning of "the natural order" in such a way that there is room for puzzlement concerning some phenomena which suggest the existence of some kind of things without their yet being integrated into what we know about the natural order. This excludes ectoplasm, phlogiston, witches, and the like, but does not (yet) exclude consciousness in general. Nevertheless, for consciousness to be a puzzle is for it to be on the verge of extinction: whatever is not (yet) clearly included in the domain of the natural order as construed by the naturalist is essentially suspicious.

The naturalistic world-view is supposed to be a safe haven because of its apparent methodological superiority over its actual and imaginary rivals. The historical background idea, which lends genealogical and psychological support to this confidence, is the notion that modernity is clearly an overall cultural progress accompanied, if not actually triggered by, an early modern scientific revolution stereotypically associated with Galileo and Newton.[11] They are seen as decisive, revolutionary cuts in the history of human thought because their discoveries reveal a gap hitherto largely covered up by an ancient, Aristotelian conception of science and nature.

The gap consists in a thorough distinction between how things appear to us as human observers of nature and nature itself. As human observers we are prone to believe that physical objects have smoothly colored surfaces regardless of how they appear to us; we believe in dusk and dawn and in heaven understood as a luminous sphere through which we can see the movement of astronomical phenomena, a sphere blue or grey during daytime (depending on whether you live in Greece or Germany) and mostly black or grey (again depending on location and season) at night, etc. Even Kant, in his famous remark that what awes him most is "the starry sky above me and the moral law in me" (Kant 2015: 129), is in the grip of a pre-modern illusion, the illusion that the starry sky is above him. Even if there were a starry sky, it would be not above him but all around him. Yet, this would make it look less transcendent, as we tend to point upwards when it comes to mysterious or awe-provoking matters, which is just a bad habit inherited from our less enlightened ancestors.

Wilfrid Sellars has notoriously named the two sides of the gap "the manifest image" and "the scientific image" of man respectively (Sellars 1963). Notice that Sellars does not speak of the manifest and the scientific image *tout court*, as he wants to emphasize that both images are systematic overall representations of how things hang together "in the broadest possible sense" (ibid.: 1) from the standpoint of a human being. There are, of course, various other ways of labeling and characterizing the gap in question: subjective vs. objective

(Nagel 1989); first-person vs. third-person perspective; thick vs. thin concepts (Levine 2004); life-world (*Lebenswelt*) and science (Husserl 1970), etc. For brevity's sake let us just speak of "the gap" in order to avoid hasty conceptualizations of the phenomena in question. Most accounts of the gap draw on a genealogical story in order to account for the alleged fact that only modern people became fully aware of it. We moderns are proud discoverers of the gap and we shun anybody who does not share our sense of it.[12]

On account of the genealogical myths which surround our modern encounter with the gap, the details of the actual story make it hard to see the conceptual core, which will play a central role in due course. Arguably all accounts of the gap rely on a background picture, which I call *standard naturalism*. Standard naturalism is really a fusion of a number of claims, in particular, a metaphysical claim, an epistemological claim, and two continuity theses.

1   (SN1) *Metaphysical naturalism (materialism)*: Everything which (really) exists is ultimately material-energetic and therefore woven into the causal web studied by our best natural-scientific practices.

2   (SN2) *Epistemological naturalism*: Everything which (really) exists can best be explained with recourse to the standards of theory construction definitive of our best natural-scientific practices.

3   (SN3) *Biological continuity*: The human brain/the human mind is part of the natural order. It is a natural kind located on a specific branch of evolution.

4   (SN4) *Methodological continuity*: Every genuine explanation has always been governed by the standards made explicit by modern science.

There are other ways of classifying the tenets built into the rather vague structure of the modern scientific world-view.[13] In what follows, I will mostly argue against (SN1) and (SN3). Yet, I believe that naturalism fails on all fronts. The human mind is not a natural kind. Only a proper subset of our mentalistic vocabulary picks out natural kinds, even though it is the case that no part of that vocabulary refers to a reality that would have existed had there been no suitable brains or other natural necessary conditions for there to be mental processes in reality.[14]

Nevertheless, let me emphasize before I get to work that naturalism is based on a wide array of actual facts that need to be respected and typically have been respected all along by many critics of naturalism. To start with, I do not intend to deny that humans are animals and, therefore, in part objects governed by the parameters articulated by evolutionary theory. Neither do I want to deny that Aristotelian physics turned out to be a huge failure. When it comes to the human mind, I am *a biological naturalist* in the sense of someone who holds that a certain type of brain is a naturally necessary condition for human mindedness, albeit not a sufficient one.[15] I am not interested in undermining scientifically established facts, but I am in the business of attacking philosophically misguided interpretations of what natural science has established and can establish in the future with respect to the human mind. Philosophically misguided interpretations of natural science are widespread, both among philosophers and among scientists.

In the next part of this chapter, I will sketch some recent arguments against naturalism, in particular against (SN1) and (SN3). I will then address the pressing question of how to conceive of the human mind after the failures of naturalism. If naturalism does not work, we need an alternative unless we are happy to accept an irresoluble riddle, a view which also has some prominent defenders.[16]

II Naturalism's Failures

Let us begin the work of questioning naturalism's claim to legitimacy with a very natural thought experiment which I will call the *New Yorker* – based on the cover of the magazine's issue for March 29, 1976, also known as "View of the World from 9th Avenue." As I write these lines, I am in Paris, which serves just as well for the thought experiment as New York. Paris is located in France, France is located on the face of the Earth, which is one of the planets orbiting the sun. When I assert these trivialities, I imagine a position from which I am able to assess claims about our location in the universe, such as Google Earth. If I press the minus button on Google Earth long enough, I get to see the Earth. There is a vantage point from which the Earth can be observed.

At this point, let us invent a much more powerful engine: Google Universe. If I press minus in Google Universe, I am in a position to observe the Earth, our solar system, its location in a branch of the Milky Way, the galaxy cluster of which the Milky Way is a part, and eventually the entire universe. But stop! Which position do I occupy when I finally reach the position from which I can assess claims about the structure of the entire universe? Certainly, I cannot coherently imagine a position from which I can observe the entire universe in a way strictly analogous to any position conceivable in a Google Earth format. The standpoint from which I observe the Earth where I am actually located while using Google Earth has a physical location at a certain distance from Earth. Yet, the standpoint from which I observe the entire universe within which I am located cannot have a physical location at a certain distance from the universe, since any such location would be within the universe. It is part and parcel of the standpoint of Google Earth that its standpoint is not on Earth, but it does not make sense to introduce a standpoint that is not in the universe, since it is part of the concept of a standpoint that we can account for its features in terms of basic geometrical and more complicated physical features built into the optical or observer-relative conditions for standpoints. What we know about standpoints is incompatible with the notion that we could conceive of a standpoint outside of the universe from which we could literally observe it.

Against this background, philosophers have criticized the assumptions underpinning the illusion of the possibility of Google Universe, which overextends the notion of a standpoint or point of view. For instance, Hilary Putnam attacks this as a "God's eye view" (Putnam 1981: 49; 1992: 7), Thomas Nagel has labeled this a "View from nowhere" (Nagel 1989), and Willard van Orman Quine denies us access to any such "cosmic exile" (Quine 1960: 275–6).

However, metaphysical naturalism or materialism seems to rely on the availability (conceivability) of a view from nowhere, as it makes claims about absolutely everything without being in a position to make justified claims about its own position within the physical totality, which is its object.[17]

At this point, the would-be materialist might resort to one of the following two options:

1 argue that Google Universe is conceivable and possible after all;
2 argue that materialism is not based on such an incoherent scenario.

Arguments for Google Universe might set out from the observation that the standpoint envisaged by Google Universe simply is our standpoint. We learn from the standpoint of Google Universe that we have a location in space-time as a whole, which can be described in terms of physics. We could apply this to Google Earth as well: if we see Earth in Google Earth, we see where we are located. If we see ourselves in the universe as a whole, we do so from within the universe. But this does not solve the problem that there is literally a standpoint from which we can see Earth and realize that we are located on Earth, whereas there is no such standpoint for the universe – at least not for the materialist.[18] Thus, this option is ultimately hopeless and unnecessarily reactive.

This is why the materialist had better choose to argue that materialism is not based on an incoherent thought experiment. At this point, she might reply that materialism is a well-established theory based on insights into the overall causal or nomological closure of the universe. The universe is supposed to be governed by natural laws and to harbor physical objects which are defined as material-energetic objects or structures and are all part of a whole, the universe, nature, or the cosmos.

Still, even on this level, materialism is a metaphysical position in at least three senses of the term "metaphysics."

First, it is a theory which claims that absolutely everything shares a set of features: absolutely everything which (really) exists is supposed to be material-energetic and governed by the laws of nature. Metaphysics is the discipline that deals with absolutely everything. It is the most universal investigation into the nature of reality, its composition, and architecture. The claim that metaphysics is ultimately futuristic unified physics can be called "physicalism" or, rather, "meta-physicalism," as it is based on a metaphysical interpretation of the nature of physics rather than on physics, as it happens to be.[19]

Second, materialism is not an empirical claim. Empirical claims are claims about the composition of specific regions of the universe. We often generalize inductively or in some other legitimate way on the basis of given data, but it is the nature of data – that is, information – that it is always limited. Here is a simple illustration of the contrast between *metaphysical* and *empirical* that I have in mind: it is an empirical fact that there are both bosons and fermions. We managed to discover this in a certain way and we have good reasons to ascribe different properties to these particles, which is why we believe that they are different. Knowing something about bosons means acquiring information, which puts us in a position to distinguish one (kind of) physical object from another (kind of) physical object. This is empirical knowledge based on information that we use in order to build a theory, which allows us to understand the basic structure of some phenomenon or other. In contrast to this empirical knowledge, to know that *all* physical objects are objects, or to know that *every* physical object is identical with itself and differs from other objects, is categorically distinct and relegates us to a different level of generality. It is hard to see what it would mean to refrain from such a knowledge claim or to base it on privileged cases (or any case at all). It carries almost no information and certainly on this level of abstraction carries no information that helps us to distinguish some natural object from any other natural object.

Materialism makes claims about all objects. In this respect, it cannot tell us anything about those objects except that they differ from other kinds of object, which according to materialism do not exist. The objects whose existence materialism rules out are the immaterial objects. Material objects do not differ from immaterial objects because they have different properties. The point of materialism is a denial of the very existence of immaterial objects. If they do not even exist, they cannot have any properties by which they can be distinguished from material objects. The materialist is not an open-minded researcher who is willing to countenance the existence of immaterial objects if someone can point them out to her, for it is extremely straightforward to do this without changing the materialist's mind. There are numbers, republics, fictional characters populating novels, movies and dreams, color sensations and beliefs, none of which are evidently material-energetic physical objects. The materialist is not moved by my insistence that there are these objects, but will immediately look out for a theory construction that allows her to eliminate these objects from a scientifically minded world-view by claiming that they have a hidden material nature. From this theoretical attitude alone, you can immediately tell that materialism is a metaphysical and not an empirical view based on actual scientific discoveries. It is in principle impossible to empirically discover the alleged fact that materialism is true, as no actual empirical discovery rules out the existence of immaterial objects.

Third, materialism is also a metaphysical thesis in that it claims to explain reality as it would have been had no one ever noticed that it is a certain way. Materialism is supposed to be a strictly theory-independent fact – that is, a fact we discover but not one we produce by having a belief to the effect that it is true. We do not make materialism true by believing that everything is material. It is supposed to be an insight into the nature of reality, one with the somewhat special status of both drawing on actual scientific knowledge and going beyond anything that could be either empirically tested or refuted.

Let me give you a straightforward example of the tensions this creates. Daniel Dennett, who leaves no room for doubt about his materialist credence, claims early on in his *Consciousness Explained*: "In short, the mind is the brain. According to the materialists, we can (in principle!) account for every mental phenomenon using the same physical principles, laws, and raw materials that suffice to explain radioactivity, continental drift, photosynthesis, reproduction, nutrition, and growth" (Dennett 1991: 33). Now, notice the suspicious exclamation mark in the quote, which at first glance seems to be an avowal of modesty. Yet, it really amounts to the stance Karl Popper labeled "promissory materialism" (Popper and Eccles 1977: 205), as the possibility of accounting for mental phenomena from a materialist standpoint is as yet far from realized.

Remarkably, less than thirty pages before this quote, in the opening argument of the entire game, Dennett argues against the anti-materialist strands of philosophy of mind on the basis of a rejection of possibilities in principle:

> One should be leery of these possibilities in principle. It is also possible in principle to build a stainless-steel ladder to the moon, and to write out, in alphabetical order, all intelligible English conversations consisting of less than a thousand words. But neither of these are remotely possible in fact and sometimes an *impossibility in fact* is theoretically more interesting than a *possibility in principle*. (Dennett 1991: 4)

I concur! However, the lesson to draw from this is that it is impossible in fact to establish the truth of materialism on the basis of what we actually know from the natural sciences. What is worse for Dennett is that within thirty pages we witness a straightforward methodological contradiction: on the one hand, our construction of a theory of consciousness is supposed to rely on an empirical spirit as opposed to "these possibilities in principle," while, on the other, that empirical stance itself is only delineated in virtue of a "possibility in principle."

So far, I have argued that metaphysical naturalism – that is, materialism – fails because it is a methodological mixture of metaphysics and empirical research. It is simply a largely unwarranted pseudo-inductive overgeneralization.

There is a second set of prominent anti-materialist arguments in contemporary philosophy. Arguments in this second set derive from the exciting interface of philosophy of mind and philosophy of language. Standard philosophy of mind deals with the *mind–brain problem* – that is, with the problem that it is very hard to see how mental items could be related to physical items and processes that fit into the natural order, such as the biochemical processes that take place within certain regions inside our skulls. Yet, one might wonder how we can actually flesh out what is so worrisome about the mind–brain problem (if there actually really is such a problem). One overall answer to this question draws on the conceptual machinery of the philosophical theory of meaning, more specifically on truth-conditional semantics. Roughly, truth-conditional semantics studies the relation between fragments of language and what they are about – between word and world, to put it in words of one syllable. In this context, one can approach the mind–brain problem via the following basic reconstruction of the conceptual machinery that creates the air of paradox constitutive of the mind–brain problem.

In his sophisticated book *Purple Haze*, Joseph Levine distinguishes two kinds of ways in which singular terms, such as nouns or descriptive phrases like "the most expensive ring in this room," can be seen to refer to the objects they pick out. One way might be called "mere labeling."[20] Mere labeling puts a speaker in *semantic* contact with some object or stuff in her environment with which she is already in *causal* contact in such a way that she puts a random label on the object or stuff without associating any explicitly available feature with the object itself. The object is *thinly* presented to her, as Levine puts it – that is, she might have all sorts of ideas about the object in question, while at the same time she is immediately in a position to grant that her ideas might be largely wide of the mark (Levine 2004: 8–9, 118–19). For instance, my use of "boson" and "fermion" in an earlier paragraph of this chapter is fairly thin, as I am by no means a trained atomic physicist. If someone who is more of an expert on particles were to tell me that I got even the basics wrong in my token use of the scientific terms, I would be happy to concede this and to revise my notions so that the result might be a more watertight use of the relevant terms. Another standard, albeit ultimately misguided example among philosophers is the identity of water and H_2O, about which no ancient philosopher had any idea.[21] Yet, this does not mean that Thales, Plato, or Karl Marx, for that matter, were not able to correctly use the words ὕδωρ or *Wasser* respectively. "Water" is just a mere label we apply to watery stuff regardless of our knowledge or ignorance of its molecular composition. The nature of water is not necessarily manifest in any competent referential use of water terms.

Levine contrasts the labeling case with the case of "thick," "phenomenal," or "substantive" concepts, as he calls them respectively (Levine 2004: 7–9). That something looks reddish to me in a certain way might also be expressed by uttering the words "This red is beautiful" or "This red is closer to purple than that other red." What we judge when we claim that assertions of this type are apt to be true cannot be judged by replacing the term with its thin counterpart. "This energetic structure with a wavelength of roughly 650 nm is beautiful" presents the object in a way that just does not lend itself to the judgment of beauty associated with the phenomenal experience of reddishness.

On closer inspection, the distinction between a thick and a thin concept does not help our case against the materialist. For, there are various materialist strategies of leveling the contrast between thin and thick referential usages of singular terms. For one thing, the contrast between water and H_2O that explains why we can learn something by figuring out that water is H_2O also relies on a thick phenomenal concept of water as watery stuff (thirst-quenching bottled water, relaxing bath water, salty sea water which reminds us of our first teenage love, or whatever). We might at first be surprised to learn that water evaporates, congeals and boils because of its molecular features when we find a hidden unity among the various surface qualities of water. But, in any event, there will be a phenomenal concept of water so that neither water nor red are mere labels. Given that we can perform materialist explanations in the thick water case (as Levine himself concedes), this undermines his case for red. If there are thin and thick usages of any term, pointing out that there is a thin usage in a given case (such as red) does not help against the materialist. At best, it amounts to a version of Jackson's knowledge argument and lands us in a different dialectics.[22] Be that as it may, Levine is after something worth keeping in mind for the constructive story to be told in the second half of this chapter. He offers a subtle semantic version of the gap, one which potentially does not motivate a placement issue per se.

David Chalmers argues prominently against materialism on a slightly different, but relevantly similar semantic basis, which accounts for the apparent distinction between the water case and the red case in different terms. Chalmers unequivocally argues "that materialism is false and that a form of dualism is true" (Chalmers 1996: xv). He defines *materialism* as "the widely held doctrine ..., which is generally taken to hold that everything in the world is physical, or that there is nothing over and above the physical, or that the physical facts in a certain sense exhaust all the facts about the world" (ibid.: 41). His much discussed *conceivability argument* against materialism can be reconstructed in the following simplified manner. First, we need the notion of a *philosophical zombie* – a physical replica of an actual human being without any inner mental life. A philosophical zombie will look just like me on the outside and on the inside, but no one will be at home, as it were. In order to make the option of philosophical zombies look slightly more plausible, imagine a scenario (a possible world) in which there is a planet on which matter regularly happens to be arranged in such a way that human observers would believe they were witnessing real human patterns there. But all there is are very stable arrangements of matter which under any possible scrutiny are indistinguishable by anyone from human beings.

Notice that Chalmers does not claim that zombies are possible in our actual world. In our world, he believes, everything which would be a physical replica of me – that is, an exact copy located in a different position from where I stand right now – would, of course, be conscious and probably in some sense have largely the same experience as I do. This is why the conceivability argument is both weaker and stronger than it appears at first glance. It is weaker in that it does not establish non-materialism for our world and stronger in that it shows that the identity of mind and matter can never be established in principle. "In our language, materialism is true if all the positive facts about the world are globally logically supervenient on the physical facts. This captures the intuitive notion that if materialism is true, then once God fixed the physical facts about the world, all the facts were fixed" (Chalmers 1996: 41). Here is a sketch of the argument, which merely serves to illustrate the basic ideas and is not intended to be the most compelling version.

i   Zombies are conceivable (the concept of a zombie does not harbor any *logical* contradiction).
ii If zombies are conceivable, they are possible (there is a

possible world where everybody is a zombie = a zombie world).

iii If brain and mind are identical, the brain–mind link is metaphysically necessary (given the metaphysical necessity of identity).

iv If the brain–mind link is metaphysically necessary, there is no zombie world.

v If materialism is true, the brain–mind link is metaphysically necessary.

vi There is a zombie world.

vii The brain–mind link is not metaphysically necessary.

∴ Materialism is false.

What is more interesting from a philosophical point of view than the actual argument, which in my view, as will come out later, is flawed beyond repair, is the technical backstage machinery called *two-dimensional semantics*. Here again the idea is quite simple and easy to follow.

There are two senses in which we use the term "water." In one sense, which Chalmers calls the "primary intension" – that is, the primary sense – "water" means watery stuff. Thales and Plato knew what they were talking about when they used ὕδωρ, even though they had false beliefs about its molecular composition, if any. If water had turned out to have a different molecular composition, say XYZ, as philosophers usually put it, Thales and Plato could still have insisted that they knew the meaning of ὕδωρ. The second sense of "water," its "secondary intension," is a function from linguistic meaning to the actual referent. The term "water" actually picks out stuff that contains H_2O molecules, and in this second sense it is necessary that it do so. Here is a simple reason for this: all identities are necessary. The fact I am I or that Mainz is Mainz is necessary, if anything is. If Mainz exists it will be Mainz, no surprise. "Boys will be boys." If water is identical to H_2O it could not have been otherwise. What this means on Chalmers's semantic construal is that we evaluate uses of "water" in two dimensions: in one dimension, where we know what we mean regardless of what the natural facts turn out to be – facts which are involved in the referential bit of our speech patterns – and in another where we take into account that water actually refers to a certain stuff with a given molecular composition. What "water" actually refers to simply could not have been otherwise than the way it turns out to be.

Given that this is a semantic model and not a linguistic claim about the actual use of water terms in various languages, dialects, or idiolects, all that we need is the *prima facie* stability of the model. It is not obviously incoherent, and Chalmers and others have defended it with respectable technical precision and detail.[23] So far, so good, then.

Chalmers now points out that, in the case of our mental vocabulary – the vocabulary in which our self-descriptions as mentally endowed conscious subjects are couched – the primary and the secondary intensions cannot come radically apart. Take as an example my impression that it feels comfortably warm in this room as I am writing this sentence. This feeling is causally hooked up with a very complex network of physical properties ranging from kinetic energy to a complicated structure of information processing triggered in my organism as a result of its surface exposure to its natural environment. Yet, it seems extremely odd to entertain the thought that the feeling of being warm could literally be an aggregate state of a natural kind which has the state of being angry at the fact that Trump won the American election as one of its parts. It looks as if we could rule this out regardless of further empirical inquiry. There seems to be no room for this option. Temperature does not suddenly change into anger so that we need an account of this process. By contrast, we know that many natural phenomena, such as the phenomena earlier called "electricity" and "magnetism," hang together and are manifestations of a single phenomenon which is only revealed once we fix the actual referents, the secondary intensions, of our earlier uninformed electricity talk. Our phenomenal experience cannot always or in principle differ radically from how things are on the level of their neural support in such a way that we could find, from the third-person perspective, that we are in a phenomenal state that is entirely different from what the subject is capable of reporting.

Chalmers thinks that his two-dimensional semantics is capable of supporting his version of the age-old Cartesian intuition that we have a privileged access to our own minds:

"We know consciousness far more intimately than we know the rest of the world, but we understand the rest of the world far better than we understand consciousness" (Chalmers 1996: 3). However, what seems really to be the case here is the reverse: if two-dimensional semantics demonstrates that there is something like a thick use of phenomenal concepts, it thereby proves that we both know and fully understand consciousness *a priori* in the relevant dimension. Therefore, there neither is a mystery, nor a great riddle, nor a hard problem. We just know consciousness from within and we fully understand it – at least on the level of our competent usage of mentalistic vocabulary along one of the two semantic axes. Given that the two cannot radically come apart according to the application of two-dimensional semantics to the brain–mind problem, there does not seem to be a further issue here.

There is a lot of wiggle room for the materialist to challenge the notion that there really is a *semantic gap* between two ways in which singular terms refer such that this gap would lend support to anti-materialist conclusions about our mentalistic vocabulary. Like Levine, Chalmers provides detailed and interesting technically sophisticated responses to some of the maneuvers that come to mind here.[24] Be that as it may, and setting some details aside, I agree with the upshot of Levine's, Chalmers's, and many others' basic idea that there is something special about our mental vocabulary, an idea that harks back at least as far as to Plato.

However, I entirely disagree with their way of locating the semantic gap within the natural order. What characteristically happens when we try to force the conscious mind with its semantic peculiarities into the natural order can be seen in roughly the last hundred pages of Chalmers' famous book.[25] Chalmers argues both for the irreducibility of the conscious mind to a non-conscious material fundamental level and for its integration into the natural order. According to this strategy, he needs to make room in the natural order for the conscious mind that *ex hypothesi* does not fit into the natural order if the natural order is exactly like the materialist wants to describe it. Hence, Chalmers resorts to the strategy of "wonder tissue" (Dennett 1991: 40), as Dennett has polemically coined moves of this sort. Like so many others over the last hundred years before him, Chalmers invokes the various interpretations of quantum mechanics as a source for possible radical revisions of our notion of the material-energetic realm in order to have space for new kinds of material entities or laws, which might then include natural laws governing additional, conscious, or proto-conscious wonder tissue.

Let me call strategies which invoke new hitherto scientifically undisclosed features of the universe in order to solve the placement problem of the mind "speculative (meta-) physics."[26] The most prominent historical representative of this strategy is Friedrich Wilhelm Joseph Schelling, who actually inspired medical science and neurobiology and was scientifically up to date in his time. Schelling also founded the *Journal of Speculative Physics*, which published articles arguably designed to widen our notion of nature so as to have room for the conscious mind and its pre-historical evolutionary stages (Schelling 2017, 2014).

In his most recent book, *Mind and Cosmos*, Thomas Nagel explicitly affiliates himself with Plato, Schelling, and Hegel and proposes a simplified version of their overall teleological account of mind's position in the cosmos.[27] Nagel indeed shares a starting point with the objective idealists, for he claims that science is bound to commit to some version of an idealist principle of intelligibility. The idealist *principle of intelligibility* generally holds that reality has to be intelligible to such an extent that we can rule out *a priori* that any far-fetched hypothesis holds which makes reality in principle inaccessible to human inquisitiveness.[28] The theory of evolution, and its actual application in various subfields of biology, assumes that its explanatory model resonates with the reality it attempts to explain. It rules out *a priori* – that is, without any application of its model to an empirically given item or structure – that nature did not come into existence five minutes ago with the traces of a far-reaching past and that, for similar reasons, Young Earth creationism or any other skeptical hypothesis can be discounted in actual scientific practice. Evolutionary theory, like any theory with obvious objective purport, relies on a match between thought and reality that guarantees there is nothing intrinsic in the reality grasped by the theory that makes theorizing inherently impossible.

Nagel rightly points out that, on closer inspection, any view about the cosmos as a whole will implicitly or explicitly draw on speculative assumptions. If this is the case, we are at the very least entitled to assume that the cosmos is not necessarily incompatible with our search for understanding and explanation. A weak version of the anthropic principle holds that the fact that there are scientific observers, such as us, tells us that the cosmos is not in principle inaccessible to thought. For thought has arisen from the cosmos itself and has managed to adapt to its laws. Any picture of human mindedness in which it is governed by laws in principle unintelligible from within human mindedness or reason will smack of unjustified skepticism.

However, after a convincing defense of the reality of reason and its irreducibility to principles external to reason (such as those discovered by evolutionary biology), Nagel jumps to the conclusion that we need a new kind of futuristic science which respects the weak anthropic principle by assuming that there is tendency in the cosmos to produce intelligent life making sense of the cosmos. Nagel happily rejoices in the romantic notion that the cosmos gradually awakens via the evolution of intelligent life until it sees itself in the mirror of human scientific practices and figures out its own existence and the place of consciousness in the world as whole.[29]

Nagel's romantic musings only make sense against the backdrop of the common assumption that any conception of the human mind must be able to integrate mental phenomena in their entirety into the natural order. Speculative metaphysics, be it of Chalmers's quantum-mechanical or Nagel's Natur-philosophical variety, is a side-effect of a conception of mind that actually views mind as something which cannot belong to the natural order as it is understood by the materialist. By trying to fit the mind into the natural order, as originally conceived by the materialist, they are granting the materialist the rules of the game, which they try to change as they play along. This incoherent sleight of hand, however, will not convince the materialist. Rather, it entitles her to postulate that, if the choice is between a fully materialistic world-view and a materialistic world-view with a magical or speculative appendix, there must be a respectable materialist theory of the mind after all.[30]

III *Geist* as an Explanatory Structure

When I gave the talk that turned into this book chapter, the majority of the audience were *awake*. Many were actually *following my argument*, trying to locate gaps and other shortcomings or attempting to *figure out* where I was leading them before they *made up their minds* about the acceptability of my claims. Every person in the room was *feeling* a certain way. Also, every person in the room *believed* that more than 300,000 Chinese households own more than one pair of shoes. Everybody who was awake during my lecture or daydreaming either *heard* my voice or *saw* my gestures, whether *attentively* or *consciously*, or at least to such an extent that each could direct the spotlight of their attention to the phenomena I was pointing out.

This is a very rough sketch of my explanation of how it is possible that a philosophical lecture was taking place at that moment in the past when I was the speaker. In addition to the aforementioned facts, there are evidently further socio-historical conditions for this event, such as the fact that belly dancing is not to be expected from the average philosopher during his talk. In the contemporary scientific climate, outrageously artistic performances, such as reading aphorisms instead of presenting thoughts in a more explicitly linear way, are also no longer to be expected from philosophers.

What I have just depicted is an explanation from the *intentional stance*, to borrow Dennett's famous term: I am giving an account of what was happening that does not mention the information processing in brains, the transformation of acoustic waves into bits of information which travel in brains through various channels. Nor did I mention gravity or any laws of nature, which are further necessary conditions for events such as philosophy lectures, as we know them.

We can now draw a preliminary distinction between *mind* and *nature* that will put us on the right track towards locating the gap that separates mind and nature without succumbing to the naturalistic pressure of locating that gap within nature. When we account for a natural kind, such as a particular hydrophobic molecule, we are warranted in believing that the natural kind might be utterly different from any specific characterization or description attached to the use of the term designed to pick it out in ordinary language. If a poet describes water pearls on the surface of a lush meadow, he is not thereby necessarily thinking of the hydrophobic properties that explain why it looks to human and other animal observers as if there were little pearls running down a surface. The phenomenon – little pearls on a surface – is very well – if not actually best – explained in terms of a natural interaction between various natural kinds. This is reflected in the notion that natural-kind terms have a potentially hidden semantic element – that is, a meaning not necessarily transparent in a competent usage of the relevant terms by ordinary speakers. The poet is not making a mistake when he describes the phenomenon; he is just not getting at the essence of the natural kind. In the poetical context, this does not constitute any sort of failure, just as the absence of poetical language in a scientific paper is rightly not perceived as a mistake.

In the case of the mind, many have pointed out that the appearance/reality distinction, the distinction between a competent surface use of a term and its essential reference, which might be hidden to the ordinary speaker, breaks down at some point. Even self-confessed materialists, such as Dennett, present their own version of the breakdown of the appearance/reality distinction for consciousness. On some level or another, in the case of consciousness, the appearance is the reality.

I propose to locate the semantic action not in a natural gap between inanimate and animate matter of a certain complexity but between natural kinds and *Geist* as an explanatory structure. To distance my account from the anti-materialist stances in standard philosophy of mind, I use the word "*Geist*" to designate the phenomena I want to characterize and to get in touch with a venerable tradition of thinking of ourselves as intelligent agents. English does not have an exact equivalent of "*Geist*," as neither mind nor spirit will really do, which is why I will stick to the German word and ask the reader to see it as a piece of technical vocabulary.[31]

The relevant distinction between natural kinds and *Geist* becomes transparent if we distinguish the following two cases of error. Imagine that I have a false belief about some natural kind. Maybe I confuse gauge and scalar bosons, since I do not really know how exactly these two types of bosons differ from each other. This does not change their essence. Gauge and scalar bosons have their individuating properties regardless of my false beliefs about them. Now imagine that I erroneously believe myself to be a leading squash player. I might have played squash with a couple of friends and observed that we were constantly getting better at the game, so I decide I will win the world championship. As I lose every single match in the tournament, I cling to my erroneous self-conception as a major squash player and explain the events as mere luck on the side of my opponent. Maybe because of some psychological feature in myself, my erroneous belief that I am a brilliant squash player evolves into a full-blown self-delusion and determines a good deal of my life.

My error about the bosons does not change the bosons. Yet, my self-delusion changes me, and in many cases self-delusion can change people to such an extent that we hardly recognize them. As a matter of fact, we build our entire lives on various forms of biased self-representation, as we all experience ourselves as centers of interest and find a location for everything we perceive or think about in various often narratively mediated accounts of who we are.[32] It is in fact impossible to account for human behavior as we know it without the dimension of our various capacities to engage in fictional story-telling. The entire socio-historical and political realm is built on our fictional capacities, which have been placed center stage in the tradition of a philosophy of *Geist* originating in the eighteenth century with Kant's "Dreams of a spirit seer" (Kant 1992). The idea in this tradition, which included Hegel, Marx, and Nietzsche and continues in a materialist disguise in philosophers such as Dennett, is that *Geist* is precisely not a natural kind because our relation to the phenomena we subsume under our mentalistic vocabulary differs significantly from our relation to natural phenomena.

Remarkably, Dennett draws a distinction between natural phenomena such as diseases and earthquakes and "phenomena that *depend on their concepts*": "On the view of consciousness I will develop in this book, it turns out that consciousness, like love and money, is a phenomenon that does indeed depend to a surprising extent on its associated concepts" (Dennett 1991: 24). Unfortunately, Dennett does not clarify to what extent consciousness depends on its associated concepts and how that differs from love and money.

And even if it is the case that elements of our mentalistic vocabulary are such that they are phenomena that depend on their concepts, we should not talk about "consciousness" here, since the umbrella term "consciousness" has uses where it actually picks out a natural kind, such as an animal's state of being awake or of having vivid hallucinatory dreams. In order to have room for a naturalization of some aspects of our self-descriptions, I want to reserve the word "*Geist*" for the features of human mindedness that really are "phenomena that *depend on their concepts*," as Dennett puts it in an unwitting Hegelian moment. For Hegel's entire philosophy of *Geist* can be summed up in the slogan that *Geist* is the domain of phenomena that depend on their concepts. The point is that *Geist* is not a natural kind or complicated structure of natural kinds but precisely something that does not even exist independently of the specific descriptions used in order to point out *geistig* phenomena. Without your belief that this is a philosophy paper, that I consciously wrote down these words intended to communicate with you, that I have read works by Dennett and that I know that there are books and objections, there would be no philosophy paper. The very existence of philosophy is clearly tied to *Geist*. Philosophy is *geistig*.

Notice that Dennett unfortunately introduces the category of what I call *Geist* only in order to head for its "extinction": "the postconscious period of human conceptualization" (Dennett 1991: 24). His brand of an eliminativist materialism, however, once again only makes sense against the backdrop of a materialist conception of the natural order, together with the assumption that human mindedness as we know it can only be integrated into the natural order or eliminated from the ontological realm of things which exist. "The idea of mind as distinct in this way from the brain, composed not of ordinary matter but of some other, special kind of stuff, is *dualism*, and it is deservedly in disrepute today" (ibid.: 33).

Sure, if *Geist* was some kind of extraordinary matter, it would deserve to be in disrepute today and should have been in disrepute at least since the dawn of philosophy. But my warranted assumptions that you are awake, that the University of Bonn is an institution financially supported by the German taxpayer, etc., are not even candidates for things composed of any kind of matter, be it regular or special kind of stuff.[33] The institution of taxes does not belong to the natural order, and we usually do not look for its integration into the natural order before we have convinced ourselves that materialism is the right kind of metaphysics and that we can only do justice to its conceptual pressures if we either eliminate or integrate into the natural order any phenomenon that does not wear its material-energetic nature on its sleeve.

It is essential to the concept of *the natural order*, as the term "the natural order" is used, that it is the order consisting of natural kinds. Natural kinds, in turn, are the kinds of things that would have been the way they are had no one ever evolved to figure out the way they are. Let us call any fact that would have obtained had no one ever evolved to figure it out a *maximally modally robust fact*. The notion of *scientific objectivity* from the third-person point of view is the notion of a position from which we are able to tell maximally modally robust facts from facts with a lesser degree of modal robustness. Precisely because we have at our disposal the concept of maximally modally robust facts, the very obtaining of different kinds of facts raises the question of whether and how these other kinds of facts might fit into the natural order. How can something that for its very existence depends on being thought of, conceived of, or experienced from a subjective point of view be part of the natural order?

The answer to this question, I suggest, is this: facts whose obtaining depends on our concepts of them as such just are not part of the natural order. However, this does not rule out that there are some relevant connections between the different kinds of facts whose obtaining we need to recognize. Yet, the relevant connections will not have any of the standard forms discussed in the philosophy of mind. Let me elaborate!

The question of how mind and brain are related to each other is utterly ill-framed. For one thing, the concept of "mind," even more than the concept of "consciousness," is a

mongrel concept.[34] It is used in indefinitely many senses and
its meaning varies grossly both synchronically and diachronically, but also according to people's beliefs about their own
mindedness. This is not surprising, because "mind" and
"consciousness," as well as the affiliated family of mentalistic
terms such as "thinking," "cognition," "will," "emotion,"
"affect," "self-consciousness," and "awareness," are introduced in large-scale explanatory contexts. For all we know
from the pictorial documents of our pre-historical ancestors,
human beings, insofar as we can know anything about what
they were up to, have been making sense of their actions in
the largest possible context of the world as a whole for a very
long time.

The pre-historical record is subject to wild mythological
speculation. It is hard enough to make sense of the mentalistic
self-portrait of Homer or the various Vedanta texts, let alone
of cave paintings, which, for all we will ever know, might
have served pretty much any function, from forms of religious
veneration to hunting manuals. The constant of mentalistic
variation is the fact that human beings are trying to make
sense of their actions within a larger context, typically within
the largest possible context they can imagine: the world as a
whole or what they believe the world as a whole to be. The
notion that mind has to fit into the natural order is nothing
but the most recent mythology, the most recent attempt to fit
all phenomena that are relevant to human action explanation
into an all-encompassing structure. What has changed over
the course of the modern development of our self-conception
is the background world-view, and not for the better!
Materialism or naturalism assumes that the world as a whole
is identical with the universe or nature and that actually to
exist is to be part of the world as a whole understood as
nature. But this move unnecessarily glosses over the fact that
the natural order in this context is invoked as an element
of action explanation. You cannot eliminate the element of
action explanation from a world-view designed to figure out
how action fits into the world, as this just undermines the
explanandum.[35]

The point about the explanandum is that it is essentially a
moving target because of its constitutive concept-dependence.
What we do is tied to how we conceive of it. Human action,

as we as historically situated agents know it, is always integrated into non-natural contexts governed by institutions. There is no point in trying to clean out the semantic mess of our mentalistic vocabulary by providing a referent from the natural order for every single mentalistic term or otherwise eliminate the term from language. The result would be not an enlightened community of scientifically minded thinkers but a society without institutions and history.

Geist is an explanatory structure invoked in the context of action explanation. Some of the things human agents do can be accounted for only with adequate reference to the fact that they do them in light of an historically variable conception of what it is for them to be human. Humans live their lives in light of a conception of what the human being is. This conception does not pick out a natural kind. One argument for this draws on the category distinction between different kinds of mistake: to be wrong about a natural kind (say fermions) does not change it. The spin of fermions is the way it is anyhow, regardless of our knowledge or error. However, if we are wrong about ourselves as agents and believe mistakenly that the human being is identical to a certain animal species to which we humans belong, this immediately changes our status as agents. Biological naturalism in the sense of an all-out identification of human being and human animal challenges our value system by suggesting a revision of our moral practices in light of its own norm. Its fundamental norm derives from the claim that to be human is to play a certain role in the animal kingdom, in the Earth zoo. This is an intrusion into the sphere of *Geist* and not a successful elimination (yet).

IV Neo-Existentialism and the Conditional Model of Mind and Brain

A proper subset of our mentalistic vocabulary comprises elements that do not refer to natural kinds. This does not rule out *a priori* that there is another proper subset of the same vocabulary that happens to pick out natural kinds. The state of being awake or various urges we consciously experience belong to this category. As things stand, our mentalistic vocabulary is differentiated both diachronically and synchronically over different natural languages and specialized idiolects. It is not unified in any specific way beyond the fact that we typically invoke it in contexts where what matters is action explanation, including activities such as predicting or regulating future behavior.

What is also important here is that our mentalistic vocabulary is not unified by constituting the body of a theory such as "folk psychology." Folk psychology is a misguided posit of theories about the human mind driven by the metaphysics of naturalism. The mentalistic vocabulary inherited from the history of literature, religion, philosophy, science, law, practices of confession, politics, etc., has only a formal core. There is no unified folk psychology that characterizes human mindedness across all speakers and cultures.

Neo-Existentialism identifies this formal core as the activity of making sense of the human being by giving an account of which faculties and conceptual capacities distinguish it both from utterly non-organic, anonymous processes and from organic non-human life. This formal core distinguishes us from all other life forms insofar as we know and understand them.

The existentialist tradition contains thinkers such as Kant, Hegel, Nietzsche, Kierkegaard, Heidegger, and Sartre. What they all have in common as a minimal assumption is the belief that *Geist*, the specifically human mind, brings with it a capacity to create institutions in light of our socially mediated map of how our actions and their explanations fit into a larger context. The human being transcends its position in any given situation and constantly integrates it into a larger cartography of how things hang together. We live our lives under the assumption that other people live their lives under different assumptions. This is why we are essentially interested in how our fellow human beings view us and reality.

Unfortunately, the existentialist tradition does not usually explicitly address the issues correlated with the mind–brain problem but, rather, offers strategies for avoiding it in justified ways. Neo-Existentialism attempts to address the issue head-on while at the same time deflating it. It argues for an anti-materialist position, as it denies that the largest possible frame in which phenomena are supposed to take place is identical to the natural order.[36] Neo-Existentialism argues that it is a misguided project to identify phenomena that essentially depend on our conceptualizations of them with phenomena unified by being phenotypes of natural kinds parsed in the terms of natural science. We should not expect that all phenomena which have been described from the intentional stance over the millennia, and for which we have some kind of record of documenting an inner life, could possibly be theoretically unified by finding an equivalent natural substratum for them.

Yet, this is arguably exactly the driving idea behind the ideology that in a recent polemical book (Gabriel 2017) I dubbed "neurocentricism." Following the British geriatric physician Raymond Tallis, I claim there that "neurocentricism" (what he calls "neuromythology") has two axes: neuromania and Darwinitis (Tallis 2014). *Neuromania*, as I understand it, is the attempt to identify the brain or, rather, its neural circuits as the natural kinds corresponding to a purified mentalistic vocabulary. *Darwinitis* is the associated attempt to explain all human behavior in terms of evolutionary biology or psychology. The concepts of "cultural evolution" and of "memes" belong to this category of mistake, since they suggest that history can be accounted for in the theoretical terms of actual evolutionary theory. While this makes for nice party jokes, I do not think that it actually leads anywhere towards explaining human mating behavior in terms of the unconscious intention hard-wired in our organisms to spread our genes, of whose existence we have become aware rather recently. As a matter of fact, integrating terms and material inferences that are valid in evolutionary theory into our mentalistic vocabulary can have the side-effect of changing us on the level of *Geist*. This is because it invites the false belief that some terminological elements that essentially do not pick out natural kinds refer to natural kinds. This is not an innocent mistake or cognitive error, for erroneous beliefs about the human mind change the status of the agent just like a clumsy squash player's delusion of being a world-class squash player turns him into a self-deluded squash player. There is a substantial difference between the fact that someone is not a good squash player and the fact that he erroneously believes himself to be one, a difference that can become the source of pathological behavior. Roger Scruton makes a similar point with respect to what he calls "biological reductionism":

> Our states of mind have intentionality and therefore depend upon the ways in which we conceptualize the world. Furthermore, we cannot assume that our emotions will remain unaffected when we learn to conceptualize their objects in some new and allegedly "scientific" way. Just as indignation at a villain is undermined by the description of him or her as an automaton obedient to impulses in the central nervous system, so does erotic love retreat when its object is described in the pseudo-scientific jargon of sexology. (Scruton 2017: 58–9)

The notion that human beings qua members of the animal realm are fundamentally or essentially biological machines whose goals are just the goals of any life form we know of is a wild overgeneralization on the basis of poor data. It only looks plausible if we ignore our historically and socio-logically mediated knowledge of the actual indefinitely large variety of human self-conceptions. Human beings essentially depend on their self-conceptions, for they act in light of who they take themselves to be.

Someone might wonder whether Neo-Existentialism is not a metaphysically extravagant view, maybe even an unwilling heir of Cartesian dualism, a creeping suspicion which typically kicks in if a philosopher opposes naturalism. In order to get a sense of why my view should not provoke this reaction, think of the relation between a bicycle and the activity of cycling. This relation offers a toy model of the ontology of Neo-Existentialism. Bicycles are clearly necessary and material conditions for cycling. No one could cycle without a bicycle (unless of course they had a tricycle ...). Now, this is hardly a profound metaphysical insight – or so I hope. Also, the physical features of the bicycle determine a range of cycling behaviors. No one could win the Tour de France with the bicycle I use to ride to my office. Yet, the relation between a bicycle and the range of cycling behaviors cannot be modeled along the lines of traditional concepts governing our understanding of the mind–brain relation. Bicycles do not cause cycling; they are not identical to cycling; cycling cannot be theoretically or ontologically reduced to bicycles; certainly, cycling cannot be eliminated by claiming that there really are only bicycles. At most, cycling supervenes on bicycles, where this just means that no cycling can take place without events materially realized at the level of bicycles. But this is not very informative, as it merely repeats the claim that bicycles are necessary conditions for cycling.

My claim is that the relation between mind and brain, in all the cases which really motivate the question of how something mental fits into the natural order, is like the relation between cycling and bicycles. The relevant *tertium comparationis* is a conditional model: the relation between mind and brain, just like that between cycling and bicycles, boils down to an arrangement of necessary and jointly sufficient conditions. There are necessary conditions for the warranted application of mentalistic terms, from talking about mere vigilance and non-conscious sensory registration to *geistig* activities such as arguing for Neo-Existentialism, thinking about the implications of monotheism for political theology, interpreting Pina Bausch's *Arien*, running for president, and so on.

Nothing that can possibly take place within the range of my organism, let alone in my brain or nervous system, could ever be sufficient for any of these activities. In fact, not even adult conscious perception falls into the category of natural kinds given its essential relation to external objects and our conceptualization of them. This does not mean that the relation between the various conditions into which we can analyze a full-blown mental situation is somehow causal. Causation only makes sense on some levels of that analysis; it does not run through all levels. Conditions for certain activities, such as exercising one's conceptual activities acquired to judge aptly that a certain wine counts as "modern" or "a smoky Washington pinot noir," include a variety of factors involving natural kinds, such as taste buds and a healthy organism. But this does not mean that my taste buds trigger the judgment that the wine I am tasting is a smoky Washington pinot noir. My taste buds stand in various causal relations (including relations with pretty much the observable universe as a whole), but this does not make it the case that their role as conditions in a network of conditions turns them into causal agents within the hierarchy of conditions.

Neo-Existentialism recommends a conditional model of mind and brain. It claims that the relationship between mind and brain is actually a relationship between conditions that we can bring to the fore only on the basis of an analysis of a given situation into its necessary and jointly sufficient conditions. This involves commitment to an indispensability thesis.[37] Our access to natural kinds works via a situation in which action explanation matters. And any such situation relies on *Geist* as an indispensable and irreducible feature.

This does not at all imply that we cannot access non-mental reality as it is in itself. Yet, it is the case that we cannot have access to both non-mental reality as it is in itself and our access conditions to it without at some point referring to real elements and processes that simply do not fall into the category of natural kinds. To know that something is the case in non-mental reality differs categorically from knowing something about this very knowledge. There are different forms of knowledge with different kinds of objectivity springing from them. To be sure, there is a general form of objectivity present everywhere where we can in principle distinguish between taking something to be true and its being true.[38] However, our concepts divide into subdomains that ideally latch onto the senses that constitute a field of sense. Different forms of knowledge require different objectivity conditions (a rule book) specified by the senses/concepts attached to a given field of sense.

Having a suitable brain is a necessary condition for participating in the explanatory structure of *Geist*. There are no immaterial souls, if this means that there are agents which interfere with the causal order studied by the natural sciences without leaving a material-energetic trace. There is no chance that I will survive my own death in any interesting sense of the term. Only some properties of me will survive my own death, such as someone's memory of me or a YouTube clip of a talk of mine. But, as Woody Allen has pithily remarked, I would rather be immortal in my apartment than in the memory of my descendants.

Yet, the fact that a brain or, rather, an entire organism, which is an instance of a species that is a link in a complicated

evolutionary chain, is a necessary condition for my partici-
pation in the explanatory, historically open structure of *Geist*
does not motivate the notion that *Geist* could find a place
in the natural order. It is simply misguided to try to fit all
phenomena into a single framework that is supposed to settle
questions of existence, or reality for that matter. Many things
are real, but this does not entail that there is a single thing,
reality, of which all real things are proper parts.

2

Gabriel's Refutation

Charles Taylor

Markus Gabriel has devised a very elegant argument to puncture the hegemony of natural science-type reductive accounts of human life, thought and action – something that I've been struggling to do myself for a few decades. In gratitude to him for this, I would like to embroider a bit around his insight.

The basic idea which excites me in Gabriel's complex many-stranded paper concerns the appearance/reality distinction (p. 34). We think of natural-scientific natural kinds as having a given nature well before we learn this or can even understand it. Water was H_2O in Thales' time, even if he saw it as (in a mysterious way) a much more widespread substance. Our knowing better hasn't changed this fact. Put another way, our learning about water doesn't change its nature.

But human experience doesn't work that way. Take our feelings, motives, reactions; we can see these as our awareness, in the mode of feeling, of the significances things and situations have for us. I love X, I fear Y, I regret Z. The fillers for X, Y, and Z are what we call intentional objects. Feelings here constitute our mode of awareness of these objects.

But this mode of awareness may undergo alteration. Take the following story: we are colleagues in a department (of philosophy, say). I tend to have a low opinion of you and find your interventions in seminars and department meetings jejune, rather flat, and unoriginal; these seem to reflect stereotypical thinking. I'd rather be elsewhere when you speak. But then I read a novel, or speak to a wise friend, or come to an understanding about some third person that she is deceiving herself. And it dawns on me that that's what I am doing. Really I envy you and can't bear that you are better than me in some significant way, so I'm always seeing what you do in an unfairly negative light.

Now this entity, my significance-drenched perception of you, is quite different from water; it doesn't stay the same regardless of how it is understood. On the contrary, it changes, it becomes other; both the significance-reading and the actual felt experience changes. It becomes something different.

We understand water better than Thales (no self-congratulation is in order; we stand on the shoulders of giants), but it's the same. In the case of my story, I understand better my feelings about you and our predicament of rivalry, but that in itself wreaks change. Before and after there are different feelings – different in an obvious sense, that they will probably bring about different action. If a third colleague asks a fourth: "Why has Taylor become less crazy? He behaves so differently when Jones is around," the other can reply: "I don't know, but he's been going to a shrink for the last six months. It must have something to do with that."

Of course, between before and after the change, there is continuity. In all likelihood, I still envy you. But the envy is now (a) consciously recognized and also (b) surrounded with an aura of shame and self-condemnation. As a felt experience, it is very different.

We can get to the point by another route. Take another case where I discover something new about myself: I've been feeling low and tired for weeks. It's getting me down. I try relaxing, reading murder mysteries, but nothing works. Then a medical friend tells me I have a bacterial infection. I get a prescription, take the antibiotics, and feel better. Here, as with water, discovering its nature doesn't change the under-lying condition – here, the infection. I do behave differently than before: I intervene by technological means to alter this condition. But this comes after, as a consequence of my under-standing what's really going on. Whereas, in the envy case, the discovery itself alters the reality I now understand better.

More generally, our understanding of the significance of things, situations, other people, the state of society – all the things we care about – plays a crucial role in what we do. You can't understand politics, culture, history, the crazy and destructive things people do, as well as the moments of insight, transformation, and increased humanity that occur, without coming to grasp the significance that all these events and situations have for the actors. Think of the catastrophic events in this new millennium which have sprung from such inadequate understanding of others.

Now this kind of phenomenon, the significance of reality R for person P, has much less definite and porous boundaries than things such as water, or conditions such as infection of the throat. How I feel about a given happening, say Trump being president, will be inflected by my sense of the significance of many other things: how I feel about the US (since I'm not a citizen of that country), how much I sympathize with my American friends, how important this setback to equal, non-discriminatory democracy will be in the world; and then, more widely, how important politics is to me, as against other things – sport, art, literature, music, travel, nature; and then my reaction will be different, if I take for granted that humanity is on a path towards more democratic equal and solidary societies, as against holding a rather low view of humans' capacities to rise above our chequered history of exploitation, domination, and massacre. And so on. (Full disclosure: I thought of myself as the reverse of naïve, with no illusions about our capacity to wreck our best achievements, but the depths of my desolation at this election gives me pause.)

Any alterations of my feelings or judgments in any of these domains, and many others which I haven't mentioned and couldn't definitively enumerate, will affect how I feel about this event. There are no phenomena of this kind which are accepted into the ontology of post-Galilean natural science. An indefinite number of other bounded phenomena could put an end to the bounded phenomenon of water – have perhaps in past time done away with this on other planets. And this kind of banishing of one by another can also happen in the domain of feelings – as when fear at a hair-raising menace utterly banishes my enjoyment of these flowers. But what

I'm talking about here: how the significance for me of reality R1 can be inflected by the significance of R2, R3, and so on, through an indefinite list – this exists only in the domain which Gabriel calls *Geist*. A science focusing on bounded realities can't come to grips with this.

Of course, all this will probably not faze true believers in reductive natural-science accounts of human life. They are looking for an explanatory reduction – the kind of thing we find in natural science, exemplified by the relation between felt heat and the mean kinetic energy of the constituent molecules. All these phenomena of experience, including the transformation of an experience's meaning through fresh insight, stands on the (as it were) felt heat side of the relationship and is explained on a deeper (kinetic energy) level through, say, changing patterns of neural firing.

To bring about a reductive account of this kind takes us far beyond our discovery that, for instance, contemplating a certain action (or observing this action in another) is accompanied by a given pattern of firing in a certain part of the brain. What we have to do to account for a transformation of experienced meaning as in my case above is to align the phenomenal change onto a neural one, and in each case explain it in part by the internal dynamic in the person (organism).

Now the dynamics at the various levels are very different, and at first blush even incompatible. The natural science account of the brain must eschew any reference to purpose or teleology. That is a condition of its being a natural science account. But any account of my transformed outlook in the above story has to invoke factors of the range of meaning, purpose, value. My radical shift in my view of you will have been triggered by something external, say, reading a novel about a person like me who was deceiving himself in similar fashion. But it is also powered by shame, by a sense of truth, and the value of truth, by some perhaps inchoate idea that I am now a better person for facing my cowardly illusions. The field in which I am changed is ethically drenched.

This doesn't by itself tell us that such a reductive account isn't possible, but we're obviously dealing with a much more formidable task than, say, correlating thoughts about X with certain firings. It is not that we cannot be deluded about our claims to act on moral considerations. My story is one such case. But to move to a level of explanation in which value considerations have no place at all is to make a much more ambitious claim. It is not entirely clear what it might look like – perhaps a radical reduction to a single amoral motivating force such as that proposed by Thrasymachus in the first book of the *Republic* ("justice is the interest of the stronger")? In any case, this is a tall program, and one whose realization, in the best case, lies far in the future. I am tempted to judge it impossible: to give an account of telic beings, like ourselves and animals, in terms cleansed of all teleology. But since any delivery on a task such as this would be at best far in the future, the promise to bring it off one day can always be put forward and cannot be definitively laid to rest.

I'm not sure I fully understand Gabriel's use of the term "Neo-Existentialist" to describe his position. At one point he invokes Sartre and his (in)famous proposition that "existence is prior to essence." But at other times he seems to be invoking a broader tradition, including among others Hegel, and it seems that he sees himself in a much broader tradition, of those that have a place for what he calls "*Geist.*"

How to characterize this tradition? We might see it in terms of the point of Gabriel's work that I picked on at the beginning of these remarks: we are made what we are partly through our attempts to understand ourselves, or the interpretations of ourselves under which we act. We don't have a nature which is just there, prior to and independent of all interpretation, like water has in its being H_2O.

But this whole life-long process of making sense of ourselves (along with human life in general) partakes of two dimensions. On the one hand, it requires invention, perhaps the production of new categories, and maybe even unprecedented ones. Seeing us through these categories changes us, as I moved in the above story, from being firmly entrenched in my immediate gut reactions to your philosophical remarks to a stance of suspicion of my own motives, from which stance my bad faith can show up. On the other hand, this self-transformation can be seen as a step towards truth, and in my story I do come to see it that way.

We remake ourselves, but how much does this remaking take us towards, or away from, our true potential? The phrase "become who you are" seems to suggest (and demand) such a progress towards a genuine identity. Hegel's notion of "truth," where the truth of something is its fully developed form, seems to suppose some such valid terminal point.

The tradition of *Geist* is one in which self-making and self-discovery can be intertwined. In this tradition, Sartre (at least early Sartre) is an outlier, in the sense that the dimension of discovery virtually disappears, and decision appears crucial. Merleau-Ponty criticizes this stance, elaborated in *L'Être et le néant*, in his own *Phénoménologie de la perception* (Chapter III.3). Back in the 1940s, the term "existentialist" was applied to the whole group around *Les Temps modernes*, including both Sartre and Merleau-Ponty. In relation to this broader definition, "Neo-Existentialist" would relate us to a broader tradition and not confine us to Sartrean decisionism.

I think this broader sense must be what Gabriel is invoking. If the "essence" of something is an inner nature which wholly determines it, as H_2O is of water, then we are not dealing with a category which can help us understand human life. We are inescapably self-determining animals. But this doesn't settle the question of the place of truth in our self-interpretations.

But one thing seems clear. The search for an adequate self-interpretation is open-ended. In that sense the expression "the world does not exist," expounded in another book of Gabriel's, is well taken. The "world," a term which for Gabriel is not synonymous with the "universe" (explored by natural science) but, rather, has overtones of Heidegger, knows no fixed limits. It is the ensemble of languages, practices, and institutions of a culture; it has a shape at any given moment (though it would take virtual omniscience to map it), but it is always being added to by new ways of understanding and living it, and, at the same time, some of its facets are falling into desuetude and forgetfulness.

So the universe (maybe) has a fixed, bounded shape – even though we may never fully grasp it. But, by its very way of being, a human culture can't be like this. If it has present limits, it can always reach beyond them. To put it paradoxically, it is in the nature of the world of self-interpreting animals like us that it is undelimitable in this fashion. To think of all of reality as bounded, as one (probably) can of the universe, is to ignore or grievously misunderstand us.

If I understand him aright, this is one of Gabriel's crucial contributions to our understanding of the human condition.

3

Does Mind "Exist"?

Jocelyn Benoist

I really feel sympathetic towards Gabriel's view on the philosophy of mind as set out in his chapter "Neo-Existentialism." His criticism of reductionism is really illuminating and his overall perspective strikes me as true.

To go directly to the remaining problem in my view, it seems to me that a further step is required: in order to make sense of the specificity of mind, maybe one should go beyond any kind of *ontological perspective* instead of trying to fix ontology. Thus, maybe, the discourse of ontology is no longer appropriate, and mind consists of nothing of which it would make sense to say that it "exists" – because by the way what would it mean for mind "not to exist"? In other words: to what does one add "mind" when one says that *there is mind* – and it can only sound as if this meant: there is mind *as well*?

To some extent, Gabriel's strategy in his text is meant to avoid this trap, because it is supposed to question not only the ontological exclusivity of physicalism but its priority as well. From the pluralistic perspective that Gabriel advocates there is no privileged sense of being; on the contrary, we have to make room for the essential plurality of the senses of being that are so to speak all on a par.

Gabriel's global purpose is to reject that formulation of the problem according to which we should find some place for mind within an essentially mindless world. We can agree on that. I still wonder whether, in his view, something doesn't remain of this problem. To be sure, according to him, there is no world, and the world that there is not is not (only) physical. However, the mental still remains something that has to be posited in contrast to the physical. Now, I am not sure that it is the best way to capture the mental. The risk, constitutive of what modernity has called "the philosophy of mind," seems then to build a mere *negative* philosophy of mind. I am not sure to what extent Gabriel avoids this pitfall.

A first possible kind of negation – which is the trouble-maker – is the negation within a genus. Then, mind would supposedly be simply *another kind* of being than the merely physical kind. Gabriel seems to reject this option in some way: "I propose to locate the semantic action not in a natural gap between inanimate and animate matter of a certain complexity but between natural kinds and *Geist* as an explanatory structure" (t/s p. 36). I take this to be right if we put the emphasis, in this statement, not on the fact that *Geist* is not any kind of matter, including an "animate" one (but what would it *mean* for it to be "matter," even so? Is such negation then *meaningful?*), but on the fact that *Geist* is not so much a *kind* as an *"explanatory" structure.*

In other words: the insistence that one finds in the chapter on the fact that *Geist* is no natural kind is certainly insightful; however, it seems that the author, in his discerning criticism of the metaphysics of mind as a "natural kind," focuses on the fact that mind cannot be *natural.* Which is certainly a fact. It seems nevertheless even more important to me that mind is *no kind at all.*

The technical term "natural kind" might turn out to be misleading. In a lot of cases it would be correct to interpret it as if its meaning depended on some preconception of "nature": thus, a natural kind would be defined as such by its belonging to *nature*, understood for example and princi-pally as the material universe. One might, however, endorse another interpretation of the so-called natural kinds: what makes them "natural" is not their belonging to a nature in a preconceived sense of the term but, rather, some semantic property such as their referential rigidity. A "natural kind" is a kind that can and should constitutively be picked out by deixis, if you want to refer to it at all. In this sense, mind could still be a natural kind without belonging to nature in the preconceived sense of the totality of what is material.

Now, the most interesting side of Gabriel's criticism of any naturalistic conception of mind, in my view, is that he seems to reject not only the claim that mind should be a natural kind in the first sense of the term, but that it is one in the second sense as well. You cannot pick out mind in this way because it is certainly no *kind*. This negation of the fact that the mind is a kind seems to me the real core of the chapter and a brilliant move. As Gabriel puts it very clearly: "Neo-Existentialism is the view that there is no single phenomenon or reality corresponding to the ultimately very messy umbrella term 'the mind'" (p. 9).

Now, if the mind is not a kind, it remains to be observed that negation cannot then have the sense that we have initially ascribed to it. It is no longer a "negation within a genus," but a *categorial negation*, which marks a categorial difference between two kinds of terms – a difference of grammar, so to speak. The grammar of mind is not the same as the grammar of nature.

It seems to me this is exactly what Gabriel is after, in particular in his beautiful toy model of cycling. "Cycling," says Gabriel, "cannot be ... reduced to bicycles" (p. 43). This is perfectly true, but not because these are entities of different sorts – different "kinds" to be precise – but because cycling – as opposed to bicycles – is not an entity. It does not have the same grammar as bicycles: from this point of view, the simple fact that it is a gerund should not go unnoticed.

As a matter of fact, *prima facie*, something or even a lot of things don't seem to work in this comparison. It seems really difficult to say that "the relation between mind and brain, in all the cases which really motivate the question of how something mental fits into the natural order, is like the relation between cycling and bicycles" (p. 43). Because, in the first place, a bicycle is the *tool* with which I cycle, whereas it is probably a bad metaphor to call the brain a tool, as if I purposefully make use of it – it is true that English speakers might say "Use your brain!" – but the metaphor, like any metaphor, should not be taken literally. But also especially because, *prima facie*, "mind" and "cycling," as terms, do not belong to the same category. The logical comparison, it seems, should rather be between *thinking* and *cycling*. This ostensible impropriety, however, reveals something:

that is to say, that mind, or at least "*Geist*," has no other substance than thinking. There is no *Geist* except insofar as it is involved in an activity. From this point of view, cycling – as opposed to the bicycle as a *thing* – might prove a good model, after all.

One might even take a step further and assert conversely that every "activity" in some privileged – and structuring human life – sense of the term is "*geistig*." Cycling, for instance, could then turn out to be an expression of *Geist* as such – exactly inasmuch as it is not reducible to the bicycle with which it is performed. This claim could be absolutely true insofar as in cycling the bicycle is *used* and use is something that never goes without *Geist* – a point that might be substantiated by the fact that, on some understanding of the word "use," it makes sense to talk of "use" insofar as there might be a *good* and a *bad* use, or at least this use might be described as more or less "*correct*." Then *Geistigkeit* certainly seems in order.

Now, the real question is whether the talk of "*Geist*" can ever make sense independently of this framework. Is there "*Geist*" independently of any "activity"? As Gabriel puts it, *Geist* being "an explanatory structure for action," it does not seem to be possible.

Now, this hypothesis is very appealing, because putting the emphasis on the activity as such in the first place helps the philosophers avoid any reification of *Geist* and, secondly, might make *Geist* altogether more concrete – give it a less ethereal ring. I am not sure, however, that a new kind of essentialization is not to be found in this characterization.

To be sure, as opposed to the "mind," *Geist* is not an umbrella term, to the extent that – this is my hypothesis – it does not mix up *notions of different categorial status*. In this regard the shift made by Gabriel's analysis from the disparate concept of "mind" to the more precise – at least categorially homogeneous – concept of *Geist* is a real step forward. However, *Geist* is still a notion that applies to a diverse range of attitudes or capacities, not all of which can be adequately captured by the term "action" – unless one holds that thinking something is itself an action, or at least for an action's sake, which, even at the cost of the broadest understanding of action, is not evident at all. Those who say that, in order to be "*geistig*," action does not need the external contribution of a thought – that *per se* would be no action – but that action *itself* is *geistig*, certainly have a point. However, this does not amount to a denial that there might also be thought without any framework of action, and that thought in this sense, as such, is *one side* of what "*Geistigkeit*" is.

In this regard, Gabriel's definition of *Geist*, apparently linking it up essentially with action, maybe seems rather too narrow. Of course this depends on how one understands "action." However, if you stretch the concept of action too much, you risk ending up with a meaningless concept – one that makes no difference, for instance, between action and simple thought, which might not be so desirable.

It remains that placing the emphasis on action probably helps the philosopher make sense of the distinction between nature and *Geist* – to put it in these terms – as a categorial one, and not only a difference between two kinds. Action is certainly no kind of entity. It is not *given* as entities are; it *is* only as far as it is to be *done*.

On the other hand, when one takes a closer look at the way in which Gabriel draws this categorial distinction, some questions might arise. It seems to me that, even if he absolutely correctly relativizes the role of "consciousness" in the delineation of the mental (or, more exactly, of the "*geistig*"), because "consciousness" is indeed an umbrella term that also covers "natural" phenomena, he still tends to determine the sphere of "*Geistigkeit*" by *self-consciousness*. Of course, both points are consistent, as Gabriel can perceive from the tradition of German Idealism that self-consciousness is precisely to be distinguished from the simple fact of consciousness. The pain in my knee is analytically conscious, otherwise it would be no pain; this consciousness, however, has the status of a purely natural, as it were "meteorological" event, to be observed. That is not what self-consciousness is about: self-consciousness is about my capacity, for instance, to treat this pain as something that happens to me, that is part of the sense of my life. Now, self-consciousness, as a principal definition of *Geistigkeit*, has its own issues.

Why should I say that the philosophy of *Geist* presented in "Neo-Existentialism" is essentially, in the tradition of

German Idealism, a philosophy of "self-consciousness"? Because of the pivotal role that self-deception plays in the way in which Gabriel articulates the aforementioned categorial difference. The basic argument is that self-deception is not a mere observational mistake. In this, Gabriel is certainly right. The difference is that the mistake I make about fermions – or indeed about anything: that is the way mistakes work – does not change fermions or what they are about, whereas my self-deception changes myself.

This is very true, but it raises some questions.

The emphasis on self-deception is a very good move, because it discloses the gap that is always potentially there between what is "*geistig*" and itself. What is "*geistig*" has essentially this capacity to be and not to be itself, whereas what is not *geistig* – but "natural" – is just what it is. In this regard, what is *geistig* always bears in itself a constitutive distance to ontology: it never comes down altogether to *what it is*.

Now, one possible *mistake* – there is one – would consist in ontologizing this distance to ontology: in saying that the *geistig* being, by the simple fact that it believes itself to be what it is not, becomes what it is not, and that finally it is what it is (that is to say: what it is not). It is obviously not true. To adopt Gabriel's example, it is not because I believe I am a squash champion that I am one. The belief doesn't actually make me a squash champion.

It remains that I do believe that I am such a champion, and that this belief is certainly part of me – and may even positively structure my existence. As a matter of fact, this is the classical move, typical of the so-called modern philosophy of self-consciousness, that Gabriel makes in his turn. Perhaps I have not become a squash champion, but I have become someone who believes he is a squash champion.

Now, to believe one is a squash champion is not the same kind of property as actually being a squash champion. Or, more exactly, *in some way* it is a property, but then it is a property like other properties – a part of what may be called my (psychological) "nature" – and *in some other way* it is not a property at all, just a semblance of a property.

In this regard, there is something very specific about these determinations that might indeed be called "spiritual" – that is to say, that they are not merely facts but also *claims*, assessable as such and justified or not. I have certain beliefs, and it is probably part of my "nature" to have them. However, it is part of the definition of these beliefs that they are or are not correct. The things might be as we believe them to be or they might not. Otherwise they are not beliefs but, again, like the pain in my knee.

This means that what *Geist* adds to nature as such is not a strange kind of thing that has the equally strange property of being able to determine what it is independently of any norm but, on the contrary, normativity as such. The things are what they are – that is their definition. On the other hand, we can be wrong about what they are, and we can even be wrong about what we are – the point being that to be wrong is still a mode of that very particular way that we have of "being," because it is a way *of existing under a norm*, which is not the same as mere "existence."

To be sure, at this point, we should introduce something like reflexivity. Normativity is, however, an essential condition of this self-reflection. Self-deception certainly is not merely a mistake. But there is self-deception only where there is *a norm to be abused*. Without the priority of the norms, there is as little logical room for self-deception as for mistakes.

In Gabriel's text, this fundamental normativity of *Geist* does not seem entirely prominent. It is more implied than made explicit. This might create misunderstandings. From this point of view, it seems to me, for instance, that the insistence on fiction – "fictional story-telling" as a central feature of *Geist* – demands a proviso. It is perfectly true that the capacity to fictionalize is an essential feature of *Geist*. However, one should then go into the grammar of fiction and observe that there is only fiction in contrast to a discourse that is not fictional – i.e., to the norms of this discourse, bracketed within the fictional discourse so as to set up another normative framework. Fiction is no mere cancelling of norms: it essentially feeds on them and plays with them, which is still another kind of normativity – a game is nothing but pure norm.

A mistaken use of the reference to fiction, and to intentionality in general, is possible – that is to say, a purely ontological reference, as if the question were only of "what there is" and not also of what norms are used. Then, one would believe that by adding fiction one adds something to our world – this mistaken belief is precisely the target of Gabriel's criticism at the beginning of his chapter. Now, fictional being is not just an additional being; fiction is an additional *norm* which does not simply add an extra nature to the realm of natural being but, rather, determines another normative framework for being – which framework makes sense only in relation (in contrast) to being in a non-fictional sense.

To overcome naturalism, as Gabriel reminds us many times, it is not just to add another – or many other – compartment(s) to natural being. Shouldn't we then proffer this alternative agenda: to open up our sense for the diversity of the senses of being, as *normative* senses?

4

Human Life and its Concept

Andrea Kern

1

The concept of a human being, according to Gabriel, is not the concept of a natural kind. The reason for this, Gabriel thinks, is that "human beings essentially depend on their self-conceptions, for they act in light of who they take themselves to be" (p. 42). Nevertheless, Gabriel thinks, "humans are animals" (p. 19).

In what follows I will argue that Gabriel's position has difficulty making sense of the latter thought. His account of the human does not allow him to make intelligible the thought, entertained by a human being, that a human being is an animal. However, if a human being cannot understand herself as an animal that possesses the very capacities in terms of which she is supposed to *understand* herself as, and hence *be*, a human being, then there is no such thing as a human being, on Gabriel's account, and hence no such thing as the various phenomena subsumed under the term "*Geist.*"

I will suggest that there is a way to keep much of the spirit of Gabriel's account of "*Geist*" without running into difficulties comprehending the thought that a human being is an animal. However, this requires that one does not think of a human being's animality as a "condition" of "*Geist.*" Rather, the animality of human beings has to be conceived as a distinctive manifestation of "*Geist,*" or so I will argue.

2

Gabriel draws on a philosophical tradition (including thinkers such as Kant, Hegel, Marx, and Nietzsche) which he characterizes by the common attempt to insist on the *sui generis* character of the feature that makes human beings unique, and which he calls, in accordance with the tradition, "*Geist.*" He thinks the most general characterization of this feature is to describe it as a "domain of phenomena that depend on their concepts" (p. 36). Proponents of this tradition typically use the term "intellect" or "understanding" or "reason" to designate this unique feature that distinguishes the human categorially from the rest of the animal kingdom. They share with Gabriel the idea that there is no single phenomenon or reality corresponding to this term but, rather, an indefinite variety of manifestations of it.

In what follows I will not address the question whether the tradition Gabriel invokes forms a homogeneous corpus with respect to the issue at stake. I assume he would agree that it does not. I will, rather, invoke another philosophical tradition in order to raise doubts about Gabriel's manner of cashing out the *sui generis* character of "*Geist.*" I am thinking of the Aristotelian tradition, which denies that a human being's animality is a "condition" of "*Geist.*" Proponents of the Aristotelian tradition rather think that a human being is *nothing other* than a certain kind of animal. Let's call this the identity claim. Gabriel thinks that, for a position to do justice to the *sui generis* character of "*Geist,*" it must deny the identity claim. Aristotelianism does not deny the *sui generis* character of "*Geist*"; rather, it denies the above conditional.

3

Gabriel defines mental phenomena by two criteria:

1   Mental phenomena are phenomena whose unity resides in the fact that they result from the "attempt of the human being to distinguish itself both from the purely physical

universe and from the rest of the animal kingdom"
(p. 10).
2   Mental phenomena are phenomena that are dependent on
    the concepts under which they fall.

In virtue of the first criterion, the concept of a human
being enters into the definition of the mental. This raises
the question as to the nature of the concept of a human
being that is employed in this definition. Let's imagine the
concept of a human being is the concept of a natural kind,
as Gabriel understands "natural kind." Then the subject of
the "attempt" to distinguish itself from "the purely physical
universe and from the rest of the animal kingdom" would be
something whose existence and identity is independent of the
concepts that articulate what it is to be a human being. This,
according to Gabriel, defines a natural kind. For a natural
kind is such that something of such a kind can fail to agree
with any specific description attached to the ordinary use of
the term with which "the ordinary speaker" identifies that
kind (p. 34).

If the concept of a human being that enters Gabriel's
definition of mental phenomena were the concept of a natural
kind in Gabriel's sense, then human beings might fail to agree
with any specific description attached to the ordinary use of
the term "human being." Now, the specific description that
is attached to the ordinary use of the term is its description
as a being who has the capacity to think of itself, and specifically to think of itself as something that differs from "the
purely physical universe and from the rest of the animal
kingdom." If the concept of a human being were a natural-
kind concept in Gabriel's sense, we would have to allow for
the possibility that human beings do not have the capacity to
think of themselves and to conceptualize themselves in this
manner. However, this would undermine the possibility of
accounting for mental phenomena in terms of this capacity in
the way that Gabriel suggests. Therefore Gabriel denies, and
is committed to denying, that the concept of a human being
is a natural-kind concept.

So let us suppose that the concept of a human being does
not describe, in Gabriel's sense, an element of "the natural
order" but something of a different kind: an item which,

according to Gabriel's definition of the term, is dependent on its concept. This is how Gabriel must think of it when he describes the life of human beings in the following way: "Humans live their lives in light of a conception of what the human being is. This conception does not pick out a natural kind" (t/s p. 41). I take this to mean that the term "human," which figures twice in this phrase, is a natural-kind term in none of these uses. When a human being lives her life in light of her conception of a human being, then she does not live her life according to a natural-kind concept. However, this raises a question that was at the center of a debate among those who belong to the idealist tradition with which Gabriel wants to associate himself. The question that was at the center of their debate, most notably between Kant and Hegel, is the question of how those who live their lives according to a conception of what a human being is can understand the thought that they, in living their lives in that manner, whatever else they are, are also a kind of animal. How do those, of whom it is said that they live their lives according to a conception of what a human being is, know that a human being, whatever else it is, is an animal of a certain kind?

Hegel blamed Kant for thinking of a self-conscious being as a being that, fundamentally, thinks of herself not as a *living* being but as a merely *thinking* thing.[1] The fundamental thought that this self-thinking being has of itself is the thought of an "I," which, as Kant emphasizes, is a "simple, and in itself completely empty, representation."[2] The thought that this self-thinking thing is a power that *can* be actualized in "various phenomena" is not necessarily contained in the fundamental thought that this self-thinking thing has of itself. Rather, it is a thought that this self-thinking thing has qua being *dependent* upon sensible conditions.

According to the Kantian picture, a self-conscious being's thought that its existence and identity is dependent upon sensible conditions is not something that it entertains qua being self-conscious. For it is not self-contradictory to think of an infinite intellect, as Kant understands this term, whose thought is not bound by the manifold that it thinks, since, on the contrary, this manifold is brought about by it. The infinite intellect, as Kant defines it, has an original intuition of objects (*intuitus originarius*) – "i.e., one that can give itself the existence of its object," which is "a mode of intuition which, so far as we can judge, can belong only to the primordial being."[3] Thus, that she who thinks "I" thinks of herself as dependent upon sensible conditions is not a thought that she has qua self-conscious being. Rather, what she thinks of herself qua self-conscious being does not exclude the possibility that she who thinks this thought could be independent of such conditions.

Self-conscious beings, according to this view, come in two varieties: one that is dependent upon sensible conditions and one that is not. Since the thought of its dependence on sensible conditions is not a thought that the dependent variety of self-consciousness has of itself qua self-consciousness, its dependence on sensible conditions must be, and hence must be thought of as, a *limitation* of its self-consciousness. According to this view the human intellect, when it thinks of itself as a distinctively *human* intellect, must think of itself as something that is *enabled* by sensible conditions that the intellect can only come to know empirically.

Consequently, a human being does not, qua being self-conscious, have knowledge of the sensible conditions of its existence and identity, let alone knowledge of the fact that it belongs to a "certain animal species" (p. 39). A human being does not, qua being self-conscious, know that she who is self-conscious exists in the sensible world, let alone that she exists as a human being. That is, a human being is, in principle, incapable of knowing that she falls under the very concept according to which she lives.

Hegel thinks that this picture is deeply dissatisfying. He argues that it contradicts the very idea of a consciousness that is nothing other than what it is a consciousness of – i.e., self-consciousness. Hegel concludes that it is wrong to conceive of self-consciousness as a capacity which, in order to fully account for itself, would need to *presuppose* the existence of something other than this capacity, namely a "certain animal species." A conception of self-consciousness that presents it as a consciousness that is dependent upon such a presupposition, he thinks, must be a misconception.[4]

Gabriel's position, I think, is vulnerable to a similar worry. The worry can be expressed as follows. If it is right to think, as Gabriel does, that "we humans" "belong to a certain animal species" with which we, at the same time, are not "identical" (p. 39), then the question arises as to how "we humans" come *to know* what "we" ourselves are. This question matters for Gabriel, because he characterizes a human being in terms of a being who lives her life according to a conception of what it is to be a human being. Thus, for there to be a distinctively human being, there must be a living being that has a conception of the human – i.e., of what it is to be a human being – under which she brings her life. This conception of the human under which she brings her life must entail the thought that a human being, whatever else it is, is a kind of living being. For, otherwise, she who lives her life according to such a conception could not bring her *life* under this conception and conceive of her life as an instantiation of it. However, this makes urgent the question of how "we humans" come to have this conception of a human being (according to which it "belongs to a certain animal species") that we, indeed, *must* have if our life has the form that Gabriel ascribes to it. Some passages suggest that Gabriel thinks of this conception as a piece of empirical knowledge. For example, when he writes: "I do not intend to deny that humans are animals and, therefore, in part objects governed by the parameters articulated by evolutionary theory" (p. 19), and then continues this phrase by saying: "I am not interested in undermining scientifically established facts" (ibid.).

This suggests that, according to Gabriel, the fact that a human being is a kind of animal is a "scientifically established fact" that we humans happened to find out. It could thus well have happened that, for whatever reason, we humans had never scientifically established this fact. However, if we humans had never scientifically established the fact that a human being is a kind of animal, then there would never have been a living being that had a conception of a human being under which she could bring her life and, hence, there would never have been a human being in the first place. For, according to Gabriel, one cannot be a human being without living one's life according to the concept of a human being; and one cannot live one's life according to the concept of a human being without thinking of a human being as a kind of animal. For otherwise my conception of a human being could not be that "in light" of which I live; it could not be that which orients or guides my life in the manner that Gabriel describes. Because it would then be logically impossible for me to think of my life and its activities as something that instantiates the very conception in light of which I live. Only the conception of a human being that entails that it is an animal of a certain kind can guide or orient my life and its activities in a manner that enables me to think of my life and its activities as an instantiation of it. For my conception of a human being to enable me to bring my life and its activities – such as, for example, my breathing and digesting, my sleeping and being awake, my perceiving and desiring, etc., – under it in a manner that entails that I think of my life and its activities as an instantiation of this very conception, my conception of a human being must entail the thought that a human being, whatever else it is, is a living being, a kind of animal.

Thus, by Gabriel's own lights, the thought that a human being "belongs to a certain animal species" cannot enter a human being's thought on empirical grounds – e.g., as something that has been established by science. Rather, since all mental activity, including scientific activity, according to Gabriel, is defined in terms of the *human* capacity to distinguish the human being "both from utterly non-organic, anonymous processes and from organic non-human life" (p. 40), it would have been logically impossible ever to establish this fact. This suggests that he must think of it as a fact that is concept-dependent – that a human being "belongs to a certain animal species" that has a place *in* the natural order is not itself a fact *of* the natural order but depends on a conception of what a human being is.

However, this option is equally unavailable to Gabriel. The fact that a human being "belongs to a certain animal species" cannot be a concept-dependent fact in Gabriel's sense because the existence of a human being is already presupposed in his account of what it is to be concept-dependent. Thus the fact that a human being "belongs to a certain animal species" can be neither a natural fact nor concept-dependent in Gabriel's sense.

I cannot see how Gabriel can avoid this dilemma. His position cannot account for the intelligibility of a human being's thought that a human being is an animal of a certain kind. Yet, at the same time, his account of the mental presupposes the intelligibility of this thought. Kant never found a solution to it.

4

In his *Encyclopedia*, Hegel remarks at the beginning of his treatment of "*Geist*" that contemporary accounts of "*Geist*" have no speculative content. "For this reason," he writes, "the books of Aristotle on the soul ... are still the most excellent, or rather the only work of speculative interest on this object" (Hegel 2010: §378). In the remainder of this chapter I will expose concisely what it would mean to treat "*Geist*" in the Aristotelian manner that Hegel praises in this passage. Aristotelianism, as will become clear, does not think that one has to give up the identity claim in order to hold on to the uniqueness of the human in terms of its mindedness. Rather, to think of a human being is to think of nothing other – nothing more and nothing less – than a distinctive kind of animal.

Thus, a human being is identical to a kind of animal, yet it is a *distinctive* kind. This is so because the vital activities of humans have a "form" that the activities of non-human animals do not have: they have the "intellect" as their "form."

As will become explicit in what follows, Aristotle thinks that, in order to account for the uniqueness of the human, it is not enough to draw a formal distinction between natural-kind facts and concept-dependent facts; rather, this distinction must have its place in the description of formal differences between different kinds of living. Aristotle formally distinguishes between three different kinds of living in terms of what he calls "soul." He defines a "soul" as the form of a living being qua living being. It is that which answers the question "What is it by virtue of which this is a living being?" The Aristotelian idea of a "soul" is the idea of a form of life among which, he thinks, we can distinguish three different kinds. Aristotle calls them the vegetative life form, the animal life form, and the rational life form.

Before we can get a sense of the manner in which Aristotle draws the relevant distinctions, I want to highlight two things that – in the context of our topic – are significant for what it means to think about the human in terms of a difference in "form." First, it means to think of this difference not in terms of certain *capacities* that a subject does or does not have but, rather, in terms of the *principle* in virtue of which certain capacities form a unity that constitutes a *subject* that can have, or not have, certain capacities. This entails a denial of a widely shared manner of thinking about the human: the idea that it is possible to account for the human in terms of an animal that, in addition to being an animal, possesses some further power such as the intellect or the power to conceptualize itself. This idea, I think, also underlies Gabriel's conception. Second, and relatedly, it means that the concepts that designate the vital operations of the living, such as eating, drinking, digesting, perceiving, reproducing, sleeping and being awake, etc., do not have a *determinate* meaning unless their principle of unification has been specified. This entails a denial of a manner of thinking about life that characterizes both the positions that Gabriel forcefully criticizes and his own approach: it is the assumption that there is a determinate sense of what it means to be a living being that equally describes the life of a rose or the life of a rabbit or the life of a human being. Rather, *what it means to be a living being*, according to Aristotelianism, is determined differently by the three different "forms" that constitute a form of life.

Aristotle expresses this by saying that "life is said in many ways" (*De Anima*, 413a20f). According to this line of thought, the concept of life, taken as such, is an abstract concept of a unity of capacities that cannot be applied to any given living being without a specification of the principle in virtue of which those capacities belong to one and the same subject. The concept of life is abstract in that, according to Aristotle, it does not contain more than the thought of a unity of capacities and activities that *explain the existence and identity* of the living thing that falls under it. It is an abstract concept because it does not contain any specific conception of the shape that this explanatory relation takes in any given case. For example, it does not tell us which capacities and activities explain the existence and identity of a rabbit, which evidently differ from the ones that explain the existence and identity of a rose, which, in turn, differ from the ones that explain how a human being comes to be.

It follows that, although this abstract characterization is true of all life form concepts, we cannot apply this abstract concept of life to any given living being without specifying the shape that this explanatory relation takes in any given case by specifying the *principle* in virtue of which its capacities and activities form the unity of a living being whose existence and identity they explain. To be sure, any living being has the power of nutrition and reproduction. And there is a kind of life that has no more than that, which is the life of plants. Animal life is different from plant life in that it also has self-movement and perception. However, it would be a mistake to think of animal life as a species of vegetative life which has powers in addition to its vegetative powers. Rather, animal life is a formally distinctive kind of life in that the principle that unifies the capacities and activities *to one and the same subject* whose existence and identity they explain is different from the one that pertains to the explanation of the existence and identity of a plant.[5] A vegetative form of life is one that does not, qua form of life, contain a differentiation between, on the one hand, an *individual* that manifests the relevant life form and, on the other, the life form itself. In vegetative life there is just constant vital activity, constant growing in all directions, all the time, and hence nothing that reflects a logical distinction between a principle of activities that pertains merely to an individual of that life form and a principle of activities that pertains to the life form itself. The activities of the life form and the activities of the individual entities that make up this life form, as Aristotle argues, are logically the same. Therefore a plant cannot be conceived as an individual being – i.e., something that manifests a principle of activity that is logically different from the one of its life form.

Animal life is formally different. Animals instantiate their life form through perception. This modifies the logical relation in which an animal stands to its life form. A subject that instantiates its life form through perception constitutes itself as a unity that is *logically different* from the unity of the life form that it instantiates. It constitutes itself as a *particular* unity and thereby distinguishes itself from the *general* unity that constitutes its life form. It is for this reason that Aristotle thinks that it is only within animal life – i.e., *perceptual* life – that the category of a *living being* can be applied. Animal life is the life of living beings. Take a lion as an example. A lion sees a particular antelope and, because of his perception of this particular antelope, this particular lion does what lions in general do when they see an antelope: the lion tries to catch it and eat it. Its life activities are *particular manifestations* of the lion form of life in virtue of being grounded in perceptions of particular things of that form of life.

Human life is not animal life. Human life differs from animal life in that it is rational. And, just as it is wrong to think of animal life as vegetative life plus some further powers that are added to this kind of life, it would be equally wrong to think of rational life as animal life plus some further powers added to this kind of life. Rather, rational life is a formally distinct kind of life. Bearers of a rational form of life instantiate their form of life through "intellect."[6] This, once again, modifies the logical relation in which a human being stands to its life form compared to the logical relation of a non-human animal. A subject that instantiates its life form through "intellect" constitutes itself as a unity that is both *logically different* from the unity of the form of life that it instantiates and *identical* to it. This is so because the power of the intellect is distinguished from the power of perception in that the content of this power is not something particular that manifests the life form, as in perception, but something general, namely the life form itself, or, as we might say, its concept. Thus, the bearer of a rational life form constitutes herself as something particular in virtue of having a conception of her life form that she takes herself to manifest. The meaning of the concept of life thus undergoes a further shift.

A subject who actualizes her life form through a conception of it constitutes herself as a unity that she takes to be a *particular* manifestation of something *general*. In this sense she constitutes herself as a subject that is both logically general and particular, and hence is both *identical* with the life form as well as *different* from it. A rational form of life is thus one that is, qua life form, bound up with forms of consciousness that represent the life form as something that is manifested in the life of its bearers. It is a life form that would not exist in the first place if its bearers did not manifest *forms of consciousness* which represented themselves as manifestations of it.

The fundamental meaning of the concept "human," according to this line of thought, is to designate such a rational form of life. It designates a rational form of life *because* there are forms of employment of the concept "human" that reflect, in various ways, such forms of consciousness.

5

The Aristotelian conception of "*Geist*" has no room for the above dilemma that, I think, should worry Gabriel. Gabriel thinks he can make use of the idea of a human being in order to account for what it is to be a "concept-dependent fact." This makes his position vulnerable to the dilemma that a human being can only be conscious of herself as a human being if she denies that a human being is, in whatever sense, a kind of animal. If a human being, by contrast, thinks of herself as a kind of animal, then she who thinks this thought is incapable of ever knowing that she is a human being. Aristotelianism does not object to the idea of a "concept-dependent fact"; rather, it employs it in its account of the "form" of a distinctive form of life. The human life has a distinctive form in that its existence and identity is dependent upon forms of consciousness whose bearers represent themselves as manifestations of the human form of life.

"*Geist*" is, indeed, an "explanatory structure" (p. 39), as Gabriel puts it. Yet, it is one that has its home in a wider explanatory structure: the one that is contained in the concept of life. It specifies the determinate shape that this "explanatory structure" takes when the life form is conceived not as something whose existence and identity is a *given* fact for those who manifest it, as it is in the case of plant life or animal life, but as something that is what it is in virtue of being known by those who manifest it. There is thus no room for being troubled by the question of how a human being can possibly know that she is a kind of animal. A human being knows what she is (and what she is not) in virtue of being what she is.

5

Replies to Jocelyn Maclure, Charles Taylor, Jocelyn Benoist, and Andrea Kern

Markus Gabriel

I Reply to Maclure

In his introduction to the present volume, Jocelyn Maclure raises different questions concerning the shape of Neo-Existentialism's take on the mind–brain problem. In this context, he emphasizes the similarity of my remarks on this topic to families of views he calls "externalist" (such as enactivism, extended mind, etc.). At the same time, he diagnoses a *prima facie* compatibility of my views on that matter with "non-reductive physicalism," "property dualism," and "emergentism" (p. 5). For reasons he hints at in his introduction, he himself generally prefers a "reasonable naturalism" to an all-out rejection of the naturalistic program.

In my reply to Kern, I will elaborate on the claim that the mind–brain (or mind–body) relationship, if anything, has the form of what I call "conditionalism." As far as we currently know, it seems to be an empirical fact that many of the activities we subsume under the heading of the mental – including (phenomenal) consciousness – are correlated with some parts of the brain. Notice that it is an empirical fact too that it is not the brain as whole which supports mental activity as characterized by most accounts of the mark of the mental having to do with consciousness.[1] Only some parts of our brain and only a subset of their activity are significantly correlated with mental activity at all. It is important to bear in mind here that it is far from clear if there actually is a neural correlate of consciousness, say. There are many reasons why there is a problem here.

One major issue is that the term "consciousness" has many usages. We first need to figure out which of them is philosophically coherent enough to be correlated with anything in the reality of our brains. And, even to the extent to which we are actually in possession of a clarified concept of consciousness, there is no unanimously accepted answer to the question of what, if anything, the neural correlate of consciousness would be – not to mention the additional problem that our brain is only one species of nervous system that might support consciousness in the animal kingdom.

Let us imagine for the sake of the argument that something like Tononi and Koch's IIT (Integrated Information Theory) is the road to a consciousness meter – i.e., to a scientifically rigorous way of identifying the neural correlate of consciousness. I have no overall conceptual reservations concerning the possibility of finding a neural correlate of what Tononi calls "consciousness," which is a kind of mental state in which we find ourselves both when awake and when dreaming. Figuring out the philosophical details of Tononi's notion of consciousness is an exercise worthy of attention. Neo-Existentialism in this context gives us some clues, but it does not immediately predict the right account. Evidently, there is much more work to do when it comes to spelling out a theory of consciousness in line with the Neo-Existentialist proposal.

There are other terms, such as "perception," that cannot have a neural correlate even in principle. At most, *conscious* perception necessarily involves the neural correlate of consciousness as identified by the best empirical theory (IIT, global workspace theory, or what have you). Clearly, some tokens of types we pick out with our mentalistic vocabulary are such that they have a neural correlate. Tononi and Koch use the term "support" here, which is even more neutral than "correlate." Some events that count as *geistig* by Neo-Existentalist lights are clearly such that they are supported by some neural events.

I happen to subscribe to the view that the human being is necessarily incarnated. Every human being, among other things, is an animal. The best explanation of our animality in my view is natural science. What it is to be an animal of a certain kind is a function of where we are located on our branch of the evolution of species. This is an element of naturalism. Neo-Existentialism (like good old existentialism) has no sympathy for vitalism, let alone for an immortal soul keeping our bodies alive for the time being.

Generally, I agree with Maclure's reasonable naturalism that we philosophers should not fumble around with scientific knowledge. Concerning scientific knowledge (which is not limited to the natural sciences), the experts count. To be sure, the frontiers of science and metaphysics are not so easily drawn. Science often makes tacit metaphysical and conceptual assumptions. This is why we cannot merely outsource the question of the human being to the natural sciences plus the humanities. The issue as to what extent human mindedness is necessarily incarnated depends on the notion of mindedness at play.

Evidently, the Neo-Existentialist account of an irreducible concept of *Geist* does not settle all versions of the mind–brain, mind–body, or mind–matter problem. In this regard, I propose conditionalism as a new candidate in the debate. According to conditionalism, any event that qualifies as mental is a whole that consists of conditions that form its parts. These conditions are necessary and jointly sufficient for the event to take place. As far as human mental activity is involved, some of the necessary conditions for any exercise of human mindedness can be identified with neural events. No brain, no mental activity. Yet, this does not support any identity theory of mind and brain; it supports only the identification of some necessary conditions of human mental activity with natural processes that are best thought of in terms of natural kinds.

However, that does not mean that the whole of a mental event is in each case best accounted for by breaking it down to a list of its necessary natural conditions. Mental events are not typically reducible in this way. Some are; some are not. This is why the issue of reductionism is ill-posed in a framework which assumes that there is one thing, "the mind," on the one hand, and another thing, "the brain," on the other, such that we can ask how they are related. In reality, there are events that we pick out with different vocabularies, including a mentalistic vocabulary. Neo-Existentialism makes claims about the roles this vocabulary plays and how naturalism is a misguided approach to some of the central roles of mentalistic vocabularies.

Most standard options spelled out in the mind–brain debate in the philosophy of mind turn out to be reifications of the participants' preferred chunk of a given mentalistic idiolect (most often: some anglophone dialect or other). There are cases where a mental event consists wholly of natural kinds, despite the fact that it is embedded in a larger context of significance. Think of the manifold cultural practices surrounding human puberty in the past and present. Puberty is a form of hormone change that can best be explained by biology. However, its behavioral manifestations play a role in human history so that the natural kind "puberty" is integrated into a larger context of *Geist*. Other cases, such as perception or knowledge, are objectively existing relations between an animal, a (Fregean) sense, and a scene comprising facts and objects. Perception is, thus, no serious candidate for an identity theory of mind and brain, say. Perception cannot be identified with any kind of neural activity, as it essentially involves the objects it is about. Typically the objects of perception are not themselves neural events.

In my view, we are currently a long way from having a complete enough understanding of the universe (qua object domain of natural science). This is why physicalism and emergentism are mere speculations. Some philosophically minded scientists happen to argue against metaphysically naturalist interpretations of current scientific knowledge and have worked out views that are even sympathetic to modern forms of full-blown Platonism, Spinozism, monadology, or Hinduistic monism. Respecting science includes respecting scientists. The fact that some of the natural scientists who achieved most (including Einstein, Schrödinger, and Heisenberg) interpret the metaphysics of science in a way utterly incompatible with the physicalist or naturalist mainstream in current theoretical philosophy does not speak in favour of the latter.[2]

The upshot of these remarks, bluntly, is that there is no single mind–brain, mind–body, or mind–matter problem. One of the many mistakes which underlie substance dualism and its ilk is precisely the thought that reality consists of two halves: the mental and the material. The question as to how the two halves are related is as ill-posed as a meta-physics which divides the universe into two parts.

What is more, the ontology in the background of Neo-Existentialism breaks with the idea of the unity of reality and the subsequent placement problem for the mind. According to what I call "the no-world-view" there is no such thing as reality as a whole. The universe qua field of sense under investigation by our natural sciences is arguably not unified either. Yet, I grant the unity of science to the naturalist in order to strengthen her position before the attack. If correct, my argument(s) against naturalism are therefore stronger, since they are directed against a stronger enemy, one who presumably has figured out the overall structure of the Humean mosaic.

Neo-Existentialism is an attempt to address the issue of human mindedness in an ontologically post-naturalistic framework. As Maclure rightly emphasizes, this framework is thoroughly realist. According to the ontology of fields of sense, the incoherent concept of reality as a whole and the even worse identification of reality as a whole with the object domain of the natural sciences need to be replaced by a better theory of reality. The ontology of fields of sense which I have spelled out and defended elsewhere claims to offer an enhanced understanding of reality as irreducibly manifold.

As a matter of fact, this anti-metaphysical maneuver is designed to lead to a stance I call "non-transcendental empiricism" (Gabriel 2015a: 245–6). This means that the metaphysical question concerning the furniture of reality or its architecture creates a pseudo-problem that leads us astray and away from an actual engagement with scientific knowledge acquisition in the real world. The rejection of naturalism associated with this project is, thus, intended to be a science-friendly stance, one designed to engage with philo-sophical problems that arise from within science. Naturally, these include problems currently dealt with in philosophy of mind, such as those surrounding the question as to whether there is a hard problem and similar riddles.

Neo-Existentialism supplies a framework for rethinking the foundations of the philosophy of mind. Once in place, it is bound to deliver verdicts on more specific problems. It draws on ontological pluralism. Hence, there cannot be an overall mind–brain problem. If anything, there are many different such problems that need not even have the same shape.

Yet, there is a sense in which Neo-Existentialism as formulated in my contributions to this book offers slightly more than merely a framework for clarifying issues that arise elsewhere (at the intersection of the special sciences and the frontiers of scientific knowledge acquisition). For Neo-Existentialism is a thoroughly non-naturalist and non-reductive position with respect to *Geist*. According to this position, it is impossible in principle to put a halt to the open-ended proliferation of ways in which we can be human. Human mindedness is actualized in many ways and in such a manner that we cannot identify a privileged substantial vocabulary that would be the silver bullet for the mind–brain, mind–body, or mind–matter problem. There just is no single such problem.

Let me conclude my reflections on Maclure's introductory remarks with a short comment on "existentialism." There are many elements Neo-Existentialism borrows from prominent existentialist thinking about human subjectivity, or *réalité humaine*, as Sartre put it. The two main components that structure the view as sketched in this volume are

1 the claim that the human being is an existence without an essence; and
2 the thought that the human being determines itself by changing its status in light of its self-understanding.

The aim of my present contributions to the development of Neo-Existentialism as an option for the coming post-naturalistic era of philosophical theorizing has been to work out some consequences of these existentialist slogans for the philosophy of mind. The plan is to reframe the central problems of philosophy of mind, which is urgently needed given the deadlocks and pathologies of the naturalist world-view still widespread among philosophers.[3]

Having said that, I surmise that the spirit of the project is perfectly compatible with a reasonable naturalism in the sense of the desire to live a modern life – i.e., a life not avoiding acceptance both of our scientific knowledge of the vastness of the universe and of our impressive ignorance of the very same universe, despite the almost equally impressive progress in scientific knowledge we have witnessed over the last two hundred years in the wake of the Enlightenment.

II Reply to Taylor

As far as I can tell from his present contribution and from my knowledge of his impressive oeuvre, there is no significant overall disagreement over the matter at hand between Charles Taylor and me. I generally agree with the thrust of his summary of the line of thought laid out in my chapter. Nevertheless, he phrases some of my claims in such a way that prompts me to clarify them. I will use this occasion to do so in response to Taylor's reflections about them.

Taylor's entry point in my Neo-Existentialist account of *Geist* is an emphasis on the role of significance in human life. Significance arises in human society on the basis of our mutual (mis)understanding of the purposes of each other's actions. We interpret what others do in light of a vocabulary that is available to us as actors, and we do this on the basis of a structured account of what we take to be the best (kind of) action or range of actions in a given situation or context.

Significance is tied to language use and language use has a history. This history is not shared across all speakers of a given natural language, since every speaker is always properly trained only in the use of some subset or other of all linguistic activities realizable in a community at a given stage of its historical development. Language is constitutively bound up with division of labor on various levels, as speakers respond to different situations, stimuli, and psychologically significant events with verbal behavior which leads to both a diachronic and a synchronic differentiation of a mentalistic vocabulary.

This basic hermeneutic insight can be spelled out in different ways. Taylor briefly mentions Sartre's decisionism, Merleau-Ponty's rejoinder, Heidegger's notion of the world, and Hegel's advanced account of *Geist*. These are all elements in a tradition I summarize under the broad heading of "Neo-Existentialism." Neo-Existentialism is an innovation to the extent to which it claims to apply the common denominator of the existentialist tradition to fundamental issues in contemporary metaphysics and philosophy of mind. This common denominator, in my view, is the thought, as Taylor puts it, that "we are inescapably self-determining animals." He is right to add: "But this doesn't settle the question of the place of truth in our self-interpretations" (p. 51). This addition is precisely what separates Neo-Existentialism from Sartrean projectivism, according to which self-determination is never subject to any norm of truth external to the one immediately available to the self-constituting agent.

To be self-determining is to lead a life in light of a vocabulary designed to make it intelligible to us how and why we do not merely blend in with inanimate nature or with the rest of the animal kingdom. This is my interpretation or rational reconstruction of Sartre's adage that we are condemned to be free.[4] In addition to this bidirectional anthropological difference, some (religious) agents are committed to a further distinction between the human being and God or the Gods (depending on the details of one's religion). Be that as it may, every human actor bases her self-determination at some point or other in her life and her psychological architecture on a more or less elaborate account of herself as minimally standing out from both anonymous nature (the universe) and other life forms.

The specifics of our various accounts of how to draw the line(s) between human and non-human being have consequences for the value system of the particular agent, as she draws socio-political conclusions from her understanding of herself in the widest possible context of thought and action available to her. We all have views about the set-up of human society as we know it that entice us to suggest or even impose concrete norms of behavior (maxims) onto ourselves and our fellow human beings. A human life inevitably has the shape of a recommendation concerning how to live well. For we think of ourselves as subject to some values or others, regardless of how often we actually act according to the values to which we believe we have subjected ourselves.

This is why the question of the truth of our beliefs concerning our mentalistic architecture does not settle the issue of who we want to be. We want to be a certain kind of person and thereby turn into that person. What we turn ourselves into, however, is not only a function of what we take to be true about ourselves. It is neither settled merely by our decisions nor by how we really are. Even though self-determination is not always bound by actual truth, it can always be assessed in view of, say, natural matters of fact or an enhanced understanding of the vocabulary we employ in the establishment and maintenance of our self-constitution.

Think of our relation to purely natural diseases. We are currently a long way from knowing everything about the human body, its conditions of health and illness, and so forth. The human body is and will probably forever remain partially mysterious to us on account of the complexity of its internal arrangements – not to mention the additional element of complexity that derives from the fact that human bodies are essentially part of an ecological system whose complexity is far beyond any mechanistic or transparently causally complete description.

This is part of why we can relate to bodily diseases in various ways. We can try to accept them as an intrusion of nature into the realm of *Geist*, which can turn into a heroic attitude or an acceptance of the contingencies that befall us as inhabitants of a universe disinterested in our existence. But we can also cook up all sorts of alternative explanations – ranging from the hope that we can somehow control our body top-down from our mind, to full-blown religious beliefs about the teleological nature of disease as punishment for sin, or whatever.

This is different from the case in which we set out to appropriate a certain fashionable vocabulary in order to adapt our psychological economy to newly created circumstances. Imagine someone who decides to become a dandy in the nineteenth century compared to Jerry Seinfeld's character in *Seinfeld*, who unsuccessfully tries over and over again to become a dandy. The way in which we think about a dandy is essentially part of what a dandy is. What a dandy is changes over time, because part and parcel of being a dandy is that the concept is surrounded by a complex web of expectations and intentions that defy any fully specific grasp of it. Similar things apply to other terms of human outlook that change with fashion.

There is no neutral ground from which we could reboot humanity so as to build a vocabulary from scratch that hooks us up with entities the nature of which does not depend on diachronic and synchronic variation.

This undermines the very intelligibility of attempts of the logical form of eliminative materialism and its ilk. These stories only make sense against the background of the value judgment that we ought to conceive of ourselves exclusively in consideration of the best available natural-scientific vocabulary – for some reason or other that often remains tacit in discussions of drastically reductive accounts of human mindedness.

The wish to integrate the human being once and for all into domains of thought where we are not constitutively present is just another mode of being human. As Stanley Cavell famously put it: "Nothing is more human than the wish to deny one's own humanity" (Cavell 1999: 109). Being human is an inescapable task for human beings. It is a task and not just a given because we cannot be human without a whole range of decisions we have to make on our path of becoming grown-ups. A human life consists of an indefinite number of stages we cannot characterize in a general theory (such as that of Kierkegaardian stages). There is no typical or overall course of human life. Too many social, historical, personal, natural, cultural, economic, etc., factors play a role in the contexts in which we can exercise the power of self-determination.

This power is in itself void of specific content. Yet, we constantly enrich it with content. The modes of the human being are a function of the context in which we actually think of the role of a human being. In actual contexts a human being can only be someone if she makes up her mind about what would count as a human achievement in a set of situations brought under concepts of contexts.

In this respect, I embrace Taylor's suggestion to classify my proposal in terms of a distinction between the bounded and the unbounded. However, I do not mean to imply that nature is merely a domain of "bounded realities" (p. 49). This is why I resort to a more neutral understanding of "nature" or, rather, "natural kinds." The thought in the Neo-Existentialism chapter is that "the universe" designates the domain(s) under investigation by the ensemble of our best established natural sciences. A natural science is a science whose objects are natural kinds. A natural kind is an object that does not change its properties by being thought of in a different way. Natural kinds are real patterns we find as we carve nature at its joints. The best way to do this is what we call "natural science." Natural science figures out what electric charge is, how far away the next galaxy is, how many types of elementary particles there are, what the ratio between baryonic matter and dark matter is, what role ions play in synaptic transmission, and what have you. Whatever natural science actually discovers cannot be integrated seamlessly into our self-understanding as minded, conscious, and self-conscious creatures. There is always going to be an additional step.

The reason for this, in my view, lies in the essence of natural science as empirical thought about the universe. Natural science cannot ever achieve closure. Even if we could know all the facts there are to know about the universe, we could not know that we know them all on the basis of natural science alone. In addition, we know by way of natural science that we will never know all the facts there are to know about the universe. We know from modern physics that there are limits to progress in physics that are set by the universe itself. To process information concerning the universe, the information has to reach us under the conditions discovered by physics, and these conditions turned out in the last century to be incompatible with futuristic omniscience. Physics will never come to an end at which it knows all physical facts. Even if, *per impossibile*, physics actually reached the ideal limit of inquiry, it would not be in a position to take notice of this fact. Qua empirical science, it has to keep an open mind concerning the facts in its object domain, the universe. The universe can always teach us another lesson, which evidently does not mean that we should be open-minded when it comes to far-reaching revisions of what we already know. Empirical knowledge acquisition should not be open-minded about the epistemic standing of skeptical hypotheses or conspiracy theories.

Against this background, my Neo-Existentialist account of the human mind is more ambitious than Taylor's use of it, even though this difference does not really show up at this stage of human scientific and technological development. Taylor is happy to settle with a good enough argument against general reductive accounts of *Geist*. Let a general reductive account of *Geist* be any view according to which it is actually possible (in the near or, at least, not too distant future) to replace all items in our mentalistic vocabulary that apparently do not pick out natural kinds by items that do. Taylor argues that such a program is a tall order that differs in kind from modest achievements of the form of an explanation of the natural kinds that trigger an episode of mental disorder, such as a case of Cotard delusion, which might best be explained as a structural type of neural misfiring in certain brain areas. In order to generalize on the basis of such known cases of bottom-up causation of mental disorders, one has to have an account of human mindedness that allows us to classify all sorts of vocabularies in which we couch our self-determination along the lines of specific cases where we did actually achieve some such explanation. Yet, it is hard to see how one should actually perform such a general reduction on an empirical basis. There is, thus, an explanatory gap between our overall mentalistic vocabulary, with all its synchronic as well as diachronic variations, and our empirically based research on mental functions grounded in neurobiological vocabulary.

> This doesn't by itself tell us that such a reductive account isn't possible, but we're obviously dealing with a much more formidable task than, say, correlating thoughts about X with certain firings. It is not that we cannot be deluded about our claims to act on moral considerations. My story is one such case. But to move to a level of explanation in which value considerations have no place at all is to make a much more ambitious claim. It is not entirely clear what it might look like. (Taylor, pp. 49–50)

At this point, the aim of my piece is more ambitious. I maintain that a general reductive account is impossible, even in principle. This is not merely an epistemological thesis but a claim about human mindedness as it really is. Human mindedness arises from the position of the intentional stance. But the intentional stance is nothing like an illusion or a delusion. Rather, it is part of reality.

At this stage, my no-world-view ("the world does not exist") enters the picture: the universe is not the whole of reality. Even though the universe is impressively large, it is not all there is (Gabriel 2015a, 2015b). Yet, this is not a metaphysical claim about reality as a whole, as there is simply no such thing. There is simply no domain that comprises absolutely everything. This puts conceptual pressure on any ontological reduction which claims that some phenomenon that we characterize in truth-apt statements actually belongs to a domain significantly different from where we originally located it.

This is not a conservative principle per se. As we figured out that witches and sorcerers belong to the domain of figments of human imagination, we were thereby justified in extending this ontological reduction to other cases, including elves and unicorns. But this does not generalize to rainbows, let alone to pains or consciousness. The sense in which rainbows are not what one might have expected differs significantly from the case of witches, not to mention God, the soul, or whatever candidate for reduction/elimination one might think of here.

My contribution to ontology (in the shape of an ontology of fields of sense) entails that a *metaphysical* reduction of all phenomena to one fundamental domain of objects (be they physical, mental, concrete, abstract, or what have you) fails in principle. Therefore, we should not strive (not even in principle!) for a metaphysical reduction of human mindedness in all its facets to natural kinds. This leaves an opening at first glance to have recourse to empirical knowledge acquisition and to reduce the human mind step by step. Yet, this is also impossible, as it would require a complete overview of human mentalistic vocabulary and, thus, an effective abolishment of the division of (linguistic) labor. Yet, this requirement is incompatible with the operation of knowledge acquisition in the natural sciences, which rely heavily on the division of (linguistic and scientific) labor. It does not help to introduce futuristic science here, since this move is not vindicated by actual science. In sum, neither natural science itself nor metaphysics makes any significant way towards an actual general reductive account of human mindedness.

This motivates the Neo-Existentialist to study the very attempts to work out such accounts in light of the existential projects involved. The Neo-Existentialist diagnoses any overall reductive or eliminativist philosophy of mind with a severe case of existential delusion. An existential delusion is any account of the human being that denies the fact that the bundle of mental faculties we generate by thinking of ourselves in a certain way is not a natural kind. There are different ways of naturalizing oneself in a delusional manner. The spectrum of delusions is very wide, ranging from rampant materialism to religious spiritualism. Rampant materialism basically claims that we are a pack of neurons or cells (if one wished to identify the human mind not with the human brain but, rather, with a larger natural structure that is part of a human body). Religious spiritualism is the belief that there are additional natural kinds in the universe hidden from the view of natural science, such as immortal souls that move our pineal gland or buzz around on the quantum scale somewhere in the microtubuli of nerve cells. Another kind of existential delusion is panpsychism or any other view which identifies human mindedness or one of its prominent features (such as consciousness) with extra forces in the universe on the same level as gravity or the electromagnetic force.

Let me conclude by slightly correcting one of Taylor's adoptions of my vocabulary in his helpful commentary. By denying that the world exists, I do not intend to embrace a Heideggerian account of the world, such as the one laid out in *Being and Time*, §§14–24. The human world or lifeworld, in my view, is also not unified or unifiable. What makes us human is a formal affair, namely the fact that we are agents of a certain kind: those agents that have to lead their lives in light of an account that distinguishes them from other animal agents and from non-agential nature. Humans draw very different conclusions from their self-constitution. Yet, at the end of the day we are all bound by this formal structure.[5]

III Reply to Benoist

If I see it correctly, Jocelyn Benoist raises two overall worries. His first worry clusters around my way of drawing a nature/ mind distinction. His second worry is related to the issues of self-deception and self-consciousness.

The first issue arises in the context of my rejection of a global placement problem for the mind. Benoist rightly maintains that my "global purpose is to reject that formulation of the problem according to which we should find some place for mind within an essentially mindless world. We can agree on that. I still wonder whether, in his view, something doesn't remain of this problem" (p. 53). As a matter of fact, there is a series of questions Benoist raises with respect to his suspicion that the Neo-Existentialist account of mind I offer might still be overly impressed by the placement problem, as it were. Let me divide his first worry into three sub-problems that I shall address consecutively.

The first sub-problem is the problem of negation. Benoist puts it thus: "However, the mental still remains something that has to be posited in contrast to the physical. Now, I am not sure that it is the best way to capture the mental. The risk, constitutive of what modernity has called 'the philosophy of mind,' seems then to build a mere *negative* philosophy of mind" (p. 54). He goes on to clarify why exactly he takes this to be a risk. The reason he offers is that one should not conceive of mind in contrast to the physical "within a genus. Then, mind would be supposedly be simply *another kind* of being than the merely physical kind" (p. 54). He claims that I probably agree with him on this point on the basis of a passage in my paper in which I reject the thought that the semantical difference between our naturalistic and our mentalistic vocabulary lies "in a natural gap between inanimate and animate matter of a certain complexity" (p. 34). Indeed, the nature/mind distinction should not be drawn within the genus "nature," which is what I basically say in the passage. More generally, I rebut any kind of dualism which draws a distinction within the genus of being or substance in such a way that there are (at least) two kinds of beings or substances, the mental and the non-mental kind.

Yet, the reason for this rebuttal might not be the one that Benoist himself prefers for his similar views concerning the irreducibility of the mental. Let me clarify some conceptual resources on which I draw. "*Geist*" is my term for the non-physical formal whole which we ontologically commit to with our mentalistic vocabulary. It is non-physical in that it has formal parts that cannot be picked out by a vocabulary whose reference conditions essentially invoke the idea of natural kinds as specified in my chapter. It is formal in that *Geist* is an object of thought that cannot be unearthed by investigating the universe. By contrast, a whole – such as an atom, a molecule, or a quasar – is substantial (non-formal) if it can be discovered only by empirical research into the material-energetic composition of the universe. *Geist* is an object in the formal sense of something that can be referred to with a truth-apt thought. It is not an object in the substantial sense of, say, "an obstacle to free passage."[6] *Geist* cannot be unearthed by natural science without its already being known to exist beforehand. Again, this does not mean that we are infallible with respect to the details of our *Geistigkeit* (the feature of being *geistig*, endowed with *Geist*).

One of the reasons why we are, after all, fallible with respect to *Geist* is that it is a whole which has physical or biological parts. My body is part of my *Geist*. As I write these lines, I engage in an activity that is essentially that of *Geist*, namely figuring out how to draw the line between the inanimate, the animate, and the human being. This activity involves the universe, as I could not encode information without material-energetic resources. I could also not write these lines without an appropriate brain that sustains my mental life and does not make me fall asleep right now, and so forth. Some parts of *Geist* have been taken by our ancestors not to be physical despite the fact that they were, and vice versa. I take it to be a conceptual, *a priori* truth that *Geist* cannot be entirely physical. However, the rest is open. Which elements of our mentalistic vocabulary are related to which bits of the universe and in what precise way is open to empirical research and conceptual clarification.

"Mind," "consciousness," and many other mentalistic terms are umbrella terms that refer to many things of different categories at the same time. Whatever they happen to refer to under specified conditions is going to be part of the formal whole of *Geist*. The criterion by which I distinguish between *Geist* and nature at the end of the day boils down to the thought that nature's composition is not a function of our beliefs about it, whereas *Geist*'s composition is. In this context, this means that how we draw the line within our mentalistic vocabulary between the bits that are grounded in the universe and those that are not is not merely a function of how the universe is. It never suffices to inspect the universe when trying to figure out whether something that plays an important role in our self-understanding as human thinkers is physical or not.

This is why the human being is profoundly and irreplaceably historical. Our self-understanding always shifts to some extent or other, regardless of how the universe actually is. Therefore, entire civilizations can create cultural symbolic orders that rest on false beliefs about the universe and that nevertheless have consequences for who and how they are.

Let us assume for the sake of the argument that a person we might call "Paul" does not have an immortal soul. However, Paul thinks that he has an immortal soul, and he takes the fact that he is a human thinker capable of many wonders of human thought to be evidence of an immortal soul in his region of presence. Maybe Paul is such a charismatic writer and knows so many people in cities spread around his natural environment that he convinces lots of people that they have immortal souls so that they erect a religion on this belief. Later, in the hands of an emperor, this might even turn into a full-blown nation-state, and so on. Of course, things like that have happened and are likely to be repeated, as humanity does not simply progress into its future by accepting natural-scientific truths about the neurobiology of consciousness into their self-understanding as humans.[7]

The *Geist*/nature distinction is formal. It does not carve nature or anything else at its joints. It shifts according to people's beliefs about who and what they are. Yet, it has an invariable core. This invariant is our activity of making sense of the fact that we do not merely blend in with what there is regardless of our self-understanding. However, we cannot identify any *natural* fact with our estrangement in the face of the vastness of a mindless universe. In that sense, there is a remainder of the placement problem in my view – or, rather, an echo of its motivation. I take it that its motivation is an expression of the human predicament that we are subject to normative demands that we cannot ground in anything ultimately non-human. For that reason, even God and the Gods in mythology and religion are interested in the human being and even assume human-like shape (be it in the form of an avatar in Hinduism or Buddhism, or in the shape of Jesus, the son of God, and so forth). The human being exists in the face of a question that can never be answered by digging our heels into nature.

This leads me to Benoist's second sub-problem, namely that of normativity. His preferred version of the irreducibility of the mental draws on the nature/norm distinction, which he takes to be "a *categorial negation*, which marks a categorial difference between two kinds of terms – a difference of grammar, so to speak. The grammar of mind is not the same as the grammar of nature" (p. 55). The mind is not distinguished from nature within any specific domain or being but, rather, differs from nature in category.

As Benoist maps the mind/nature distinction onto a norm/nature distinction, I understand him as committing to something along the following lines. For a suitable agent to be subject to a norm is for her behavior to be evaluable with respect to correct or incorrect, good or bad performance.[8] If an agent ought to φ, but she χs instead, she makes a mistake. What we observe is that she χs. This observation does not tell us anything about whether she ought to φ despite the fact that she is actually χ-ing. In contrast to this much invoked case of actions subject to normative assessment, the equally much discussed case of processes subject to natural laws is one in which all that matters is what happens. If a group of particles is entangled in a quantum state, their properties have to be characterized in a certain way. The particles are φ, and there is no sense in which they ought to be anything else.

An example of the normativity of the mental is the role of truth in our lives. If I wrongly believe that p, I make a mistake. But the fact that p is false is not itself a mistake. In order to wrongly believe that p, it takes more than the falsity of the proposition that p. Making a mistake cannot be reduced to a proposition's being false. We have to mistake something false for something that is true. Yet, that is also not sufficient for interesting actual cases of epistemic blameworthiness. If I make a mere guess concerning the whereabouts of Boris Johnson (say, I locate him in Oxford while he is actually in Mombasa), I do not make the same kind of mistake that I would make if it mattered to my interlocutors and me where he actually is. The truth and falsity of propositions take on a life of their own in the context of our discursive practices of ascribing epistemic states and of thereby aiming at the truth. Part of why *Geist* is not a natural kind, then, has indeed something to do with the normative dimension of human life.

Yet, however precise one makes this line of thought, it does not change the fact that mind, or rather *Geist*, exists. Normativity exists as much as fermions, galaxies, and earthquakes. Nevertheless, this specifically does not mean that there is a genus (existence) of which there are different kinds or modes, as I have argued elsewhere in detail (Gabriel 2015a: 135–56). We cannot place all there is in one big domain, for no such domain can possibly exist. Thus, ontologically speaking, it is correct "that mind is *no kind at all*" (Benoist, p. 54).

Benoist gives this thought an additional twist with which I wholeheartedly agree. He writes:

> One might, however, endorse another interpretation of the so-called natural kinds: what makes them "natural" is not their belonging to a nature in a preconceived sense of the term but, rather, some semantic property such as their referential rigidity. A "natural kind" is a kind that can and should constitutively be picked out by deixis, if you want to refer to it at all. In this sense, mind could still be a natural kind without belonging to nature in the preconceived sense of the totality of what is material.
>
> Now, the most interesting side of Gabriel's criticism of any naturalistic conception of mind, in my view, is that he seems to reject not only the claim that mind should be a natural kind in the first sense of the term, but that it is one in the second sense as well. You cannot pick out mind in this way because it is certainly no *kind*. (pp. 54–5)

In this passage, Benoist rightly generalizes on the basis of my argument in the chapter for an objection to the very idea of

a naturalistic account of mind. The historical openness of
mind makes it impossible for us to pick out and to rigidify
our mentalistic vocabulary in an attempt to close the shifting
semantic gap that separates us from the non-human regions
of what there is.

In a sense relevant in this connection, Neo-Existentialism is
committed to a bundle theory of mind. The mind is a bundle
of faculties and activities we unify in the context of action
and thought explanation. We want to figure out who we are
as human beings and how we ought to project ourselves into
the future in the face of phylo- and ontogenetic existential
threats. In this context, we make sense of our own contributions to what there is by creating a historically open-ended
proliferation of terms and inference rules that connect them.

The third and easiest of Benoist's sub-problems is related
to the very idea of an ontology of mind or *Geist*. According
to Benoist, there is a threat in "ontologizing" (p. 58) the
mental. He insists that the "particular way that we have of
'being'" consists in the fact that we exist *"under a norm,*
which is not the same as mere 'existence'" (p. 59). My answer
to this is straightforward: if we exist under a norm, this
evidently does not mean that we do not exist. *Geist*, and, as
a consequence, the mental, is itself something which there is.
It exists just like other formal objects exist. There is nothing
special about its very *existence*. Therefore, I see no overall
problem in "ontologizing" the mind.

The second set of problems Benoist formulates draws on
my claim that self-consciousness and self-deception essentially hang together. To be a self-conscious agent constituted
by one's self-understanding is a fallible stance. When we get
ourselves or others wrong, when misunderstandings occur,
we are liable to change our status as agents so that we
become self-deluded.

To be sure, self-delusion is not the only form of existential
pathology. In my chapter it serves as a paradigmatic case
designed to illustrate that each of us is the kind of object that
changes if we have false beliefs about it in virtue of the fact
that we have false beliefs about it. Here I agree with Benoist
that this presupposes that "normativity as such" is already
in play: "This means that what *Geist* adds to nature as such
is not a strange kind of thing that has the equally strange

property of being able to determine what it is independently of any norm but, on the contrary, normativity as such" (p. 59). Self-deception is, by these lights, thus an abuse of norms. It is a case of failure which presupposes that there are norms to which we are subject insofar as we aim at being human in light of our conception of the human being. But then, again, this does not cancel out an ontology of the mental. *Geist* really exists. One way in which it manifests itself is the medium of fiction. We essentially tell stories about how we became who we take ourselves to be. Human agents constitutively have autobiographies. These autobiographies are designed to make sense of the fact that we do not merely belong to nature as the domain we find in place; rather, the scene we enter is that of making sense of our lives.

What is fictional is not opposed to what exists. Fictional objects, such as autobiographical selves, exist and have real impact in our conscious lives. In this respect, to be a fictional object is essentially to be related to a mode of conceiving of that very same object in a narrative mode.[9] The difference between fictional and non-fictional objects hangs on this essential dependence. One way of summarizing my take on the ontology of fictional objects would be to say that fictional objects essentially exist in the context of an interpretation. Fictional objects depend for their existence on an interpretation of them. Without interpretation, they would have no determinate properties at all.

Think here of the notorious problem of the indeterminacy of fictional objects such as Macbeth. Does he have long hair? Does he have pets? How many pairs of shoes does he own? We regard non-fictional objects as complete regardless of how anyone thinks about them. Whatever I take to be true about the exact number of cells in a determinate region of my left elbow, there is an exact number. Yet, what about the molecular composition of Macbeth?

My reply to this problem is that Macbeth's properties can be fixed according to any interpretation that is compatible with the basic facts about him. One of the basic facts about Macbeth on any acceptable interpretation is that he is a human being. Now we know that human beings typically have many trillion cells that make up their bodies. We are, thus, entitled to interpret the play in any way compatible with the fact that Macbeth is not an indeterminate object but precisely a human being tied to an animal body.[10] We have no reason to assume that Macbeth is objectively indeterminate, even more so given that the play is supposed to be staged. The fact that Macbeth is played by an actor usually solves the indeterminacy problem by the actor's very presence on the stage. One of the many differences between Macbeth and me is that my physical properties do not vary from legitimate interpretation to legitimate interpretation. There is just one set of facts about my body that does not vary across a range of admissible imaginary variations.

Geist partakes in the fictional domain. As human agents, some of our formal parts are fictional. To be a dancer, a husband, a traveler, a friendly customer, a gourmet, or what have you, depends essentially on an interpretation. For this reason, there is a history of dance, marriage, tourism, gastronomy, and so forth. This history consists of a series of interpretations that justifiably count as admissible in their time and place. The fictional, therefore, does not contrast with the real or the existent. Rather, it is part of what there is. The fictional field of sense (which is actually not unified into one kind of field of sense, but thereby hangs a tale ...) is as real as the universe.

IV Reply to Kern

Kern challenges a core structure at the center of the conceptual architecture of my view with her formulation of a dilemma, which I will call *the anthropological dilemma*. She then sketches a view she dubs "Aristotelianism" and argues that this view is not subject to the anthropological dilemma. I will take up the issues in that order.

The motivational structure of the alleged dilemma Kern presents draws on a series of assumptions many of which I do not share. She claims that "one cannot live one's life according to the concept of a human being without thinking of a human being as a kind of animal" (p. 66). Yet, how exactly would one support this somewhat surprising claim? This claim is surprising because it seems to be presented as an empirical fact that someone cannot have the concept of a human being without thinking of themselves as an animal. Without having to delve deeply into speculative paleoanthropological or actual ethnological research on such matters, it should be clear that it is not at all hard to imagine human beings that have a conception of themselves without thinking of the human being as an animal. Suffice it to mention hard-nosed religious fundamentalists of all the stripes that define themselves by the very negation of Darwinism. Many Christians, for instance, actually believe that humans are not animals in the sense that Darwin claimed. Regardless of the actual biological facts about the human species, it should be obvious that there is a natural fact settling whether we are animals or not. What it is to be an animal, then, consists in that fact. In other words, qua animals we do indeed have an essence, an essence picked out by those biological terms that refer to a natural kind. Let us assume that current biological science roughly tracks that essence in terms of its ontological commitments to protein production, RNA, DNA, cells, and so forth. Kern certainly does not want to deny this, as she wants to subsume DNA under her Aristotelian concept of a life form.

On many accounts of the semantics of natural-kind terms, our ancestors and contemporaries, who were ignorant of these facts or respectively deny them, nevertheless refer to an arrangement of natural kinds, for they use the term "animal." Yet, they disagree with us when it comes to the question whether *they* are animals. This is why they are subject to normative evaluations from the other side of the debate concerning the question whether we are animals.

There is ample space for views that accept that humans have an animal side but that the human being is not at all animalistic. Suffice it to mention unabashed forms of ontic dualism according to which humans have an animal part and a non-animal part – say, their immortal soul.

Those who do not think of themselves as animals in the right way (whatever the right way is) make a mistake. This mistake can assume various shapes. All that Neo-Existentialism claims on that front is that any such mistake will not be a mistake merely about natural kinds but also a mistake about ourselves, as it will have severe repercussions in our self-conception as human beings. Therefore, I do not see why it should be impossible to live one's life according to a conception of the human being while being in explicit denial or simply ignorant of the fact that, as a human being, one is a kind of animal.

As a matter of fact, there is a sense in which my Neo-Existentialism makes explicit room for such an option without denying that every human being is an animal. For a human being to be an animal is not for it to be identical with an animal. As a human being, among other things, I am an animal. The meaning of "animality" is fixed by natural science. Let me mention in passing that, on my reading, Aristotle would agree and that he ought to revise his conception of animality in light of the empirical knowledge he did not possess. Were he to know what we know, Aristotle would have to change his views about animals.

Kern is right that I run "into difficulties comprehending the thought that a human being is an animal" (p. 61). But the reason for this is that I disbelieve that the human being is an animal. A human being – i.e., a case of human being – is a case of *Geist*. Nevertheless, in order for the concept of a human being to be instantiated, there are necessary natural realization conditions. Every human being is necessarily incarnated. Our incarnation is a condition of the life of the mind. Mental events have natural and non-natural parts. The whole of a mental event, however, is not natural. The whole of the human being has the shape of *Geist*. But *Geist* cannot exist without drawing on natural resources. Evidently, this does not mean that every human being knows that there are natural resources required for her mindedness. What is even more obvious is that no human being currently knows where exactly to draw the line in her life between the natural and the *geistig* parts. All that we can know from the conceptual point of view of Neo-Existentialism is that the synchronic and diachronic divergence in our mentalistic vocabularies is not a function of natural changes alone.

This allows me to accommodate the thought that our animality is "a distinctive manifestation of '*Geist*'" (p. 61) in the following sense: how we incorporate our incarnation into our self-portrait as human beings is not a natural fact, but a *geistig* one. In general, *Geist* is the capacity to draw a distinction between the human and the non-human.

In particular, *Geist* actualizes itself in specific accounts of that distinction. These accounts draw on empirical material, including existential experiences of giving birth, life, suffering, health, happiness, and death. The full array of human experience, as it is articulated in our manifold aesthetic, religious, scientific, philosophical, etc., expressions, is a manifestation of *Geist*. *Geist* necessarily has animal parts regardless of the degree to which human beings are fully and adequately aware of them.

On the basis of her disagreement with me concerning the question of whether there could be human beings who live their lives according to a conception of the human being that does not include thinking of themselves as animals, Kern formulates the following problem.

> This suggests that, according to Gabriel, the fact that a human being is a kind of animal is a "scientifically established fact" that we humans happened to find out. It could thus well have happened that, for whatever reason, we humans had never scientifically established this fact. However, if we humans had never scientifically established the fact that a human being is a kind of animal, then there would never have been a living being that had a conception of a human being under which she could bring her life and, hence, there would never have been a human being in the first place. (p. 66)

This follows only if one assumes – like Kern but unlike my Neo-Existentialism – that human beings essentially think of themselves as animals. Yet, Neo-Existentialism has room for rejecting that. What speaks in favor of the Neo-Existentialist position here are empirical facts concerning our knowledge acquisition of our animality, together with ethnological facts concerning human beings who explicitly live their lives according to a conception of the human being that excludes the concept of animality from the portfolio of their self-consciousness as humans. Now, they might be wrong (as I believe). Nevertheless, they are human beings. One of their existential problems is that their mistake about themselves affects the core of their being, as they instantiate the concept of a deluded human being. Human beings are in a fallible position with respect to themselves, including their animal parts. It could, thus, indeed, "well have happened that, for whatever reason, we humans had never scientifically established this fact" of our own animality.

In this connection, it is important to remind ourselves of the further fact that there is a host of different conceptions of our animality. As modern conceptions emerged in the eighteenth and nineteenth century there was – and still is – significant disagreement between positions such as that of Marx and Engels, Darwin, Nietzsche, and contemporary views in, say, evolutionary psychology, cognitive science, psychoanalysis, behavioral economics, and so forth. When it comes to animality, I am happy to defer to the life sciences – not because of their conceptual clarity, which is often lacking when it comes to the philosophical interpretation of their implications for *Geist*. The reason we should simply accept established scientific facts about our animality on the level of *Geist* is that they tell us something about the shifting border between the animal and non-animal parts of *Geist*. For instance, we now know that human behavior is often caused by non-conscious biochemical events for which an agent is not responsible. To be sure, our current knowledge is a long way from providing justification for reductive generalizations (Gabriel 2017: ch. 5). Nevertheless, what we find out about the human body often leads to a renegotiation of the conceptual border between the natural and the non-natural. Recognition of new borders is not necessary. When presented with conceptual change of this kind on the level of *Geist*, many reactions are possible. We cannot predict how exactly humans will take the news. After all, think of how long it took for the German legal system finally to recognize the biological fact that human animals are not born with two sexes expressed only in the exact shapes a male or a female body can take. Until 2017, human babies born in Germany were regularly mutilated on the ground that certain natural facts were not recognized on the level of *Geist* – not to mention all the further issues of race, gender, body shape, health, disease, etc., that are currently up for grabs in socio-political reality and discourse. None of these issues can be settled *a priori*. We need to bring in "established scientific facts" and figure out how to incorporate these in our self-portrait as human beings.

Neo-Existentialism charges those who do not subject themselves to the progressive forces of border renegotiation in light of the scientific progress of modernity with a mistake on the level of the human being. Neo-Existentialism is a modern stance. Nevertheless, it makes room for its own fallibility. Should it turn out that modern science produced mistakes that had relevant repercussions for *Geist* and were incorporated, we would have reasons to withdraw these mistakes from our self-portrait. This holds, in my view, for neurocentrism, as I call a certain ideology whose most famous expression is the thought that we have no free will because our animal conditions are supposed to be incompatible with the possession of such an extraordinary power (Gabriel 2017).

Kern devises another subtle version of the anthropological dilemma. She presents an argument based on her reconstruction of premises from my view designed to support the conclusion that "the fact that a human being 'belongs to a certain animal species' can be neither a natural fact nor concept-dependent" (p. 67) in my sense. Here is my reconstruction of her argument, drawing on pp. 67–8 in her reply.

P1 The thought that a human being "belongs to a certain animal species" cannot enter a human being's thought on empirical grounds, e.g., as something established by science.

P2 All mental activity is defined in terms of the *human* capacity to distinguish the human being from the non-human.

P3 It would have been logically impossible to (empirically?) establish the fact stated by P2.[11]

P4 The fact stated by P2 is concept-dependent. This means that the fact that a human being "belongs to a certain animal species" that has a place *in* the natural order is not itself a fact *of* the natural order but depends on a conception of what a human being is.

P5 The fact stated by P2 cannot be concept-dependent, because the existence of a human being is already presupposed in the account of what it is to be concept-dependent.

C The fact that a human being "belongs to a certain animal species" can be neither a natural fact concept-dependent in Gabriel's sense.

This argument cannot justifiably claim to be based on a collection of premises from my account of the human being. There are many details in this reconstruction that I do not share. Evidently, I explicitly deny P1. The only legitimate question is whether acceptance of some of the other premises commits me to P1 after all.

Here is a line of thought that could motivate me to accept a version of P2. My Neo-Existentialism departs from a two-tiered anthropological premise. This premise states (1) that there is widespread synchronic and diachronic variation in our mentalistic vocabularies and (2) that this variation presupposes a shared invariant ground. The shared invariant of human mental activity is the capacity to render intelligible the fact that we do not merely blend in with inanimate nature. As far as we know, our deep historical past is one dominated by mythological and religious instances of such an account. These accounts are not empirical in the sense that they are not attempts at explaining natural events pertaining to the universe.

The argument for this relies on my version of what I call "the gap." According to this version, the gap separates natural kinds from the human being in that the human being changes in light of its beliefs about the human being. From this line of thought I do not draw the conclusion that the human being belongs to an animal species that has a place in the natural order. Once more, I conceive of the relation between our animality and the human being in terms of a structure of necessary and jointly sufficient conditions. Our animality is a necessary condition of a whole (*Geist*) that cannot be reduced to natural conditions. Animality is not sufficient for human being. This means that there is no specific human animality. Qua animals, we do indeed blend in with the rest of the animal kingdom regardless of whether we accept this or not on the level of the human being. Qua human beings we can be deluded about our place in nature, which is a concept-dependent fact.

The fact expressed by P2 is, thus, concept-dependent. The naturalist and the anti-naturalist Neo-Existentialist disagree about human mindedness. The anti-naturalist Neo-Existentialist claims that there is no specifically human mental event that can be reduced to its natural conditions.

The naturalist disagrees. According to the Neo-Existentialist, the naturalist does not make a mistake about a natural kind but, rather, is deluded in various ways. This is why he treats naturalism as an ideology rather than as an empirical or metaphysical thesis about the universe. Naturalism is not merely false; it is a pathological form of deception.

Regardless of the details of Kern's argument, and my rejection of some of its premises as well as its motivational apparatus, it might be useful to make my stance towards the conclusion more explicit. Is the fact that a human being "belongs to a certain animal species" a natural fact or concept-dependent in my sense? Or to put this in a way more congenial to my actual position: how do we integrate the fact that we belong to a certain animal species into our self-conception as human beings? Clearly, we can account for the natural conditions of human existence in terms of evolutionary biology. We possess a certain biological equipment without which we would not be in any position to acquire perceptually based knowledge about the universe. Our bodies are selection-functions whose programs are written in biological code. To put it bluntly, I am a happy naturalist about our (and any other) animality. The human animal, to the extent to which it is an object of biological science and medical knowledge, is a complex arrangement of natural kinds, a causal web.[12]

At the same time, there is another dimension of intelligibility in which our bodies make an appearance, the field of sense of the human being. This is where my ontological background theory, the ontology of fields of sense, enters the stage. The universe (or nature, for that matter) is not all there is. The field of sense of the human being overlaps with the universe. We leave traces in the universe that are not visible from the standpoint of natural science unaided by knowledge that has a *geistig* shape. Yet, this line is not immune to empirical revisions. The overlap of the fields of sense denoted by "the universe" and "*Geist*" respectively is not a top-down affair but a hybrid of conditions that play together in contingent ways.

Let me resort to my preferred example of cycling. If I ride a bike in order to go to Koblenz, say, you can look at what takes place in the universe as this happens. This will involve knowledge of the air pressure in my tires, gravity, electric charges in neurons, radiation patterns on my retina, the other forces of the universe, and whatever might be going on at scales that are currently beyond physical knowledge. Yet, no collection of facts about the arrangement of natural kinds in that situation will ever be a complete description of what is going on as I am riding my bike to Koblenz. For one thing, the city of Koblenz involves legal concepts, a history, vague delineations of its borders, romantic musings about the Rhine, and so on. My wish to ride to Koblenz will have something to do with my sensibility to the Rhine valley on account of the fact that I grew up there. It involves my currently existing capacity to ride a bike and my knowledge of the way to Koblenz along the river's bank. It is impossible in principle to know that I am riding my bike to Koblenz on the basis of any knowledge of the universe alone. This is why Neo-Existentialism is anti-naturalist.

At the heart of this anti-naturalism is a version of an *indispensability thesis*: our non-naturalistic knowledge of the human being is an indispensable starting point for any investigation into the composition of the universe (Gabriel 2017). We simply cannot eliminate the human being from our view of what there is. Obviously, this alone does not have metaphysical anthropic consequences precisely because the universe is the domain of objects that cannot comprise the human being. We leave traces in the universe that are only visible from the standpoint of a human being, invisible otherwise.

I would like to conclude my response to Kern with some reflections on Aristotelianism, as she introduces it. First of all, I reject the identity claim, which should be obvious from both my chapter and the outlines of the present response. It is not the case that the human being is nothing other than a certain kind of animal. Kern presents the identity claim as

> a denial of a widely shared manner of thinking about the human: the idea that it is possible to account for the human in terms of an animal that, in addition to being an animal, possesses some further power such as the intellect or the power to conceptualize itself. This idea, I think, also underlies Gabriel's conception. (p. 69)

Unfortunately, in her reply she does not tell me what she takes to be the general flaw in any such additive conception, and it is not clear to me where to locate the potential for a substantial disagreement between the Neo-Existentialist and the Aristotelian. For, on one interpretation, the Neo-Existentialist is an Aristotelian after all. What I have in mind is this: if we call the whole which has animal and *geistig* parts the human life form, all parties in dialogue here are entitled to subscribe to Kern's view that

> Human life is not animal life. Human life differs from animal life in that it is rational. And, just as it is wrong to think of animal life as vegetative life plus some further powers that are added to this kind of life, it would be equally wrong to think of rational life as animal life plus some further powers added to this kind of life. (p. 71)

But that does not entail any substantial problem for the anti-naturalist Neo-Existentialist unless Kern shows that "human life" in her sense is a natural kind in my sense. For, then, she might be on the verge of vindicating a naturalistic position on Neo-Existentialist grounds, which would mean that Neo-Existentialism's claim to anti-naturalism is not fully warranted.

Generally, my preferred take on the "mind–body problem" is that mind and body are not related to each other in any of the ways standardly considered (identity of any sort, substance dualism, supervenience, grounding, etc.). The model for their relationship that I offer can be labeled *conditionalism*. Conditionalism is the view that any event that counts as an exercise of the human being's capacity to conceive of itself in light of a notion of the human being involves both mental and non-mental conditions. The non-mental, natural processes that are part of human life are not independent strata but, rather, elements in a field of sense accessible to natural-scientific knowledge acquisition about natural kinds. Hence, the *geistig* dimensions of our life are not somehow added on to a non-mental reality. They are themselves a kind of reality such that elements from non-mental reality (but not all of non-mental reality) are a part of them. *Geist* is a whole which in the case of a human being has a body as its part.

To sum up, I am not convinced that my position is really

> vulnerable to the dilemma that a human being can only
> be conscious of herself as a human being if she denies that
> a human being is, in whatever sense, a kind of animal. If
> a human being, by contrast, thinks of herself as a kind of
> animal, then she who thinks this thought is incapable of ever
> knowing that she is a human being. (p. 72)

It is not correct that *a* human being cannot think of herself
as a kind of animal. Yet, if I think of myself as a kind of
animal, I think of my body as having a certain constitution
consisting of an arrangement of natural kinds best understood by natural science. Biology knows better what an
animal actually is than any armchair reasoning about the
human life form. All I have been saying is that *the* human
being, or human being for short, is not a kind of animal
but an instance of *Geist*, where "*Geist*" does not pick out a
natural kind and is, hence, a whole that cannot be subjected
entirely to natural-scientific research.

It is also not correct that, if someone thinks of herself as
a kind of animal, she is "incapable of ever knowing that she
is a human being." All I have been saying is that someone
who thinks of herself as a kind of animal in the sense of
"animality" brought out by modern natural science makes
a mistake on the existential level. She is wrong not merely
about a natural kind, but about herself, as she thinks of
herself in terms of a vocabulary designed to pick out natural
kinds. There are various degrees of deception that can flow
from this.

Having said that, I do not believe that Kern's Aristotelian
thinks of herself as an animal in the sense of an overall
biochemical autopoietic emergent whole, or whatever is
exactly the right take on the notion of life that best captures
the spirit of contemporary biology on that matter.[13] Rather,
the Aristotelian introduces a notion of human life that makes
it hard to see how a human being can be an animal. At
the end of the day, the anti-naturalist and the Aristotelian
might converge on the issue of human animality once the
meaning of "animality" is settled in the context of the
semantic framework I assume in my account of "scientifically

established facts." It seems to me that Kern's notion of human life is incompatible with the thought that our animality is best described by the contemporary life sciences. She might then agree with me after all that human beings can think of themselves without conceiving of their humanity in terms of the (alleged) fact that we are a certain kind of animal. For this is exactly what Kern proposes under the heading of Aristotelianism.

Notes

Introduction

1 I wish to thank Jean-Philippe Marceau and Hugo Tremblay for their perceptive and relevant comments on an earlier version of this introduction, as well as Jean-Philippe for his careful editorial assistance. I am indebted to Markus Gabriel, Charles Taylor, and Dominic Cliche for the stimulating discussions over the years on the issues discussed in this volume. Markus Gabriel's contribution was first presented as the inaugural "Grande conference de la Chaire *La philosophie dans le monde actuel*" at Laval University in January 2017.

2 See Taylor (1964); "Self-interpreting animals" and "Hegel's philosophy of mind" in Taylor (1985a); and "Interpretation and the sciences of man" in Taylor (1985b).

3 See Benoist (2001).

4 Chalmers (1996).

5 Gabriel is skeptical about the concept of "cultural evolution," but there are ways to make it plausible. See Lewens (2015).

6 Searle (2010). Interestingly, Gabriel shifts from mind to action when he tries to spell out what is occluded by a strictly physicalist account of the mind. But it is not clear that even identity theorists need to deny, for instance, that "Human action, as we as historically situated agents know it, is always integrated into non-natural contexts governed by institutions" (p. 39).

7 Robinson (2017).

8 Clark and Chalmers (1998).

9 Varela, Thompson, Rosch (2016 [1991]); Noë (2009). In his new introduction to the ground-breaking book that he published in 1991 with Francisco J. Varela and Eleanor Rosch, Evan Thompson writes: "cognitive science indicates that what we call 'the mind' is a collection of constantly changing, emergent processes that arise within a complex system comprising the brain, the rest of the body, and the physical and social environment, and in which we find no single, abiding, and controlling self" (p. xx). I can easily see how Gabriel would want to challenge, rightfully in my view, the anti-realist ontology espoused by many "enactivists," but there the theories of mind expounded appear to be largely congruent.

Chapter 1 Neo-Existentialism

1 Earlier versions of this piece were presented at Mainz (to Robert Nitsch's research group in neuroscience), the New School for Social Research, Utrecht University, Paris 1-Panthéon Sorbonne, and as a "Grande conférence de la Chaire *La philosophie dans le monde actuel*" at Laval University in Quebec. Many thanks to the organizers and audience for helpful comments and discussion points, in particular to Jocelyn Benoist, Paul Kottman, Jocelyn Maclure, Robert Nitsch, and Herman Philipse. I also thank my team (James Bahoh, Marin Geier, Jens Pier, and Jens Rometsch) at my Chair in Epistemology, Modern, and Contemporary Philosophy for reading the manuscript, discussing many of the thoughts expressed here in great detail, and for editing the text. Special thanks to Jocelyn Maclure for his suggestion to publish an extended version of the original paper in the form of a discussion volume and to John Thompson at Polity for his continued support of my work.
2 This very formulation already raises many problems. What is it for an individual to be introduced? If the thought is that an individual is introduced by being referred to or mentioned for the first time in human linguistic history, then far too many objects would have to count as fictional and, therefore, non-existent. Imagine that in the future astronomers were to formulate their theories in the form of novels, such that every new astronomical object discovered was first introduced in a novel. Or think of the actual fact that a lot of clearly existing objects (including natural kinds, such as water or celestial bodies) were first introduced in fiction (mythology and so forth).
3 See, for instance, Azzouni (2010: 14):

I claim that we (collectively) subscribe to a particular criterion for what exists. This is that anything exists if and only if it's mind- and language-independent. Dream figures, fictional characters that authors have made up, and hallucinated objects are all, in the sense meant, mind- and language-dependent. Dinosaurs, protons, microbes, other people, chairs, buildings, stars, and so on are (purported) examples of mind- and language-independent objects. ... In my sense of "mind-independent" and "language-independent," no one can dictate such an object into existence by (merely) thinking it or symbolizing it as so.

I disagree. For details on existence, see Gabriel (2015a).
4 Here is how Price (2011: 187) puts it:

If all reality is ultimately natural reality, how are we to "place" moral facts, mathematical facts, meaning facts, and so on? How are we to locate topics of these kinds within a naturalistic framework, thus conceived? In cases of this kind, we seemed to be faced with a choice between forcing the topic concerned into a category which for one reason or another seems ill-shaped to contain it, or regarding it at best second-rate – not a genuine area of fact or knowledge.

5 For an introduction to this view, see Gabriel (2015b).
6 As a side note: I wholeheartedly reject the idea that there really are such things as "analytic" and "continental" philosophy. See Gabriel (2015a: xii–xiii).
7 See the famous paragraph on the meaning of "substance" in the *Principles of Philosophy*, book 1, §51 (AT VIII 24), where Descartes claims that, strictly speaking, there is only one substance.
8 For more on this, see Gabriel (2017).
9 On this, see Tetens (2015), who argues that naturalism either turns out to be a strong metaphysical claim about absolutely everything or has to remain incomplete so that there will forever be room for non-natural objects in a more complete account of what there is. If naturalism is a strong metaphysical claim, however, there is a conceptual gap between any finding of the natural sciences and naturalism. That would mean that no progress in the natural sciences should ever convince anyone of the truth of naturalism. See also the account of the relationship between science and metaphysics in Chakravartty (2017).
10 For a careful proposal along those lines, see Hofweber (2016). Hofweber convincingly argues that there is ultimately no route to unrestricted nominalism in the sense of "the view that all there is

are objects in spacetime, or all there is is concrete" (2016: 289). The primary reason he invokes for this is that "There is no list of terms in our language such that if none of these terms refer, then we can conclude that there are no abstract objects" (ibid.: 290).

11 Ed Dellian, the German translator of Galileo and Newton, has pointed out to me in correspondence just how erroneous it is to think of these two scientists as precursors of contemporary naturalism. See his account and defense of the non-reductive philosophies of nature he finds in Galileo and Newton in Dellian (2007). However, this creates the new worry that consciousness is too smoothly integrated in this kind of philosophy of nature so that we wind up with a different kind of naturalism still incompatible with Neo-Existentialism as laid out here. If we think of consciousness as built into the fabric of the universe, we still conceive of it as an entity "out there" in a way the Neo-Existentialist finds objectionable on conceptual grounds.

12 Most recently, Dennett has asked the question as to where the gap comes from in order to make it go away: "By reconceiving of the gap as a dynamic imagination-distorter that has arisen for good reasons, we can learn how to traverse it safely or – what may amount to the same thing – make it vanish" (Dennett 2017: 21). However, he forgets that the genealogy of the gap is at the same time a genealogy of the scientific world-view which gives rise both to the impression that there is a gap and to attempts, such as his, to close it or to make it vanish. For more balanced accounts of the genealogical difficulties this involves, see Blumenberg (1985) and Taylor (2007). See also Gabriel and Žižek (2009).

13 Huw Price (2011: 187, 199) distinguishes between "object naturalism" and "subject naturalism." For him, object naturalism in the sense of a metaphysical claim is a failure resulting from ignoring the subject-naturalistic fact that "the contribution on our side" in knowing something about what there is "never goes to zero" (ibid.: 30). "Science is only one of the games we play with language. Each game privileges its own ontology, no doubt, but the privilege is merely perspectival. Science is privileged "by its own lights," but to mistake this for an absolute ontological priority would be to mistake science for metaphysics, or first philosophy" (ibid.: 31). Yet, it is not clear to me why Price labels his own position "subject naturalism." In what sense is his account of the uses of language and the claim that there is no metaphysically relevant universal quantifier "naturalistic"?

14 On this, see Gabriel (2017).

15 Here "naturalism" about the human mind contrasts with "supranaturalism" about the human mind, which would be the view that some or all mental terms refer to a reality that would have existed

had there been no brains and that will exist even after all brains have vanished from the universe.

16 See the much discussed new mysterianism of McGinn (1993, 1999). See also Pinker (1997). Both draw on Noam Chomsky's claim (1975, 1988) that there are inherent limits to what we can even conceptualize on account of the structure of the human mind. Against the underlying assumption that there might be ineffable facts that we cannot even conceptualize in principle because of inherent representational limits of human language, see the conceptual idealism of Hofweber (2016: Ch. 10).

17 Remarkably, Dennett explicitly makes use of "a God's-eye view of the universe" (Dennett 1984: 101). His compatibilist account of determinism (which he aptly distinguishes from fatalism) relies on a standpoint "*sub specie aeternitatis*" (ibid.: 124) and on a thought-experiment based on the possibility of surveying all of actuality ("the actual trajectory of the world" [ibid.: 126]) in one eternal glance. However, as I have argued (Gabriel 2015a, 2015b), there is no such thing as actuality in that sense. This is not just an epistemic fact stating our metaphysical ignorance, but an ontological fact restricting what can actually be the case.

18 A theist or classical metaphysician with ontotheological inclinations could argue that God's eye view is conceivable under the condition that it does not occupy a literal point of view. The entire tradition of classical metaphysics, to the extent to which it has been sympathetic to this move, reserved a highly special observer status for a God's eye view (it was supposed to be atemporal, outside of space and time as we know them, omniscient, etc.). Naturally, these are no options for the metaphysical naturalist.

19 "Meta-physicalism" in that sense is similar to what Agustín Rayo (2013: 5–12) calls "metaphysicalism." Like Rayo's metaphysicalist, the meta-physicalist believes that there is a metaphysically privileged structure which is the real target of reference. Unlike Rayo's metaphysicalist, the meta-physicalist bases her claim on physics and not on armchair reasoning about the relation between truth, reference, and reality alone. However, the strategy of outsourcing conceptual problems to futuristic physics is certainly no better than metaphysicalism all by itself.

20 On concepts that "really are essentially labels," see Levine (2004: 165).

21 For a more nuanced and historically adequate treatment of this alleged identity statement, see Chang (2012). For a convincing alternative to the other standard (and equally misguided) example of the alleged identity of temperature with mean molecular kinetic energy, see Bishop and Atmanspacher (2011). The latter paper also includes an alternative to the physicalistic notion of a causal closure of the

physical universe under the heading of "contextual emergence." However, as will become clear in the main text, this account still counts as naturalistic by my lights, as the domains it countenances are all treated as given and located within the overarching domain of empirical research.

22 See, of course, Jackson (1986).

23 For an overview of the development of two-dimensional semantics and its application to the problem at hand, see Chalmers (2006a, 2006b, 2009). See also Jackson (1998). There are other strands and earlier precursors. The technical details will not matter here.

24 See the discussion in Shear (1997).

25 Chalmers (1996: 276–357). The strategy of reverting to quantum mechanics in order to bridge the semantic gap between the two dimensions of sense suspiciously resembles an *obscurum per obscurius*, of which Chalmers himself is aware, as he concludes his book with the admission "that *all* interpretations of quantum mechanics are to some extent crazy" (ibid.: 356).

26 Dieter Henrich (2007: 47) pithily sums up the weakness of this move in the context of an attempt to solve the placement problem by locating the mind in a hitherto hidden meshwork of material forces:

> It is not unreasonable to conclude for oneself that the subjective has to be grounded in something of the sort that at the end of the day cannot be distinguished from matter. Yet, this conclusion is a step beyond the realm of scientific research into material processes. In this way, one does not prove anything, but rather sketches and accepts a conception such that one is in a position to know that it cannot achieve the status of a demonstrable explanation. (My translation)

27 The view that rational intelligibility is at the root of the natural order makes me, in a broad sense, an idealist – not a subjective idealist, since it doesn't amount to the claim that all reality is ultimately appearance – but an objective idealist in the tradition of Plato and perhaps of certain post-Kantians, such as Schelling and Hegel, who are usually called absolute idealists. I suspect that there must be a strain of this kind of idealism in every theoretical scientist: pure empiricism is not enough. The intelligibility of the world is no accident. Mind, in this view, is doubly related to the natural order. Nature is such as to give rise to conscious beings with minds; and it is such as to be comprehensible to such beings. Ultimately, therefore, such beings should be comprehensible to themselves. And

these are fundamental features of the universe, not by products of contingent developments whose true explanation is given in terms that do not make reference to mind. (Nagel 2012: 17)

28 On this concept of idealism, see Gabriel (2016a). For a recent defense of a combination of what he calls "conceptual idealism" with a relevant denial of ineffable traits of reality, see Hofweber (2016: 248–73).

29 See Nagel (2012), for example pp. 124, 106.

30 Recently, Görnitz and Görnitz (2016) have argued that quantum theory after all is not metaphysically crazy and that it is exactly the kind of futuristic science Nagel envisions. They present a case to the effect that the right kind of metaphysics of information easily bridges the semantic gap. However, the cost of their view is that it threatens to dissolve the material-energetic realm into structures too closely resembling mental items. In other words, they tend to solve the placement issue by postulating an all-encompassing domain of information which incorporates both mind and matter as two forms that information can take. Their view, which is based on actual physics, comes uncannily close to an updated version of Schelling's objective idealism.

31 For more on this translation problem, see Gabriel (2017: 1–4).

32 See Dennett (1992). For a similar conception, see Gabriel (2017: 166–9). The difference is that I connect the phenomenon of the center of narrative gravity with the Freudian notion that the function of the game of giving and asking for reasons is to justify our emotional stances with respect to others. In this way, I avoid the various traps of a narrative account of personal identity familiar from Ricoeur (1992).

33 In his Locke Lectures, Dennett defines dualism as "the idea that minds (unlike brains) are composed of stuff that is exempt from the laws of physical nature," and without any counter-argument ridicules it as "a desperate vision which richly deserves its current disfavor" (Dennett 1984: 28). For one thing, which genuine dualist ever claimed that mind was made of any stuff? And even if Plato and Descartes, say, had believed that mental substances were composed of immaterial stuff (which they did not), why would anyone have to add that this additional stuff has to be entirely "exempt from the laws of physical nature"? Dennett's rejection of dualism falls prey to the procedures of a very primitive intuition pump in his own sense of the term. His anti-dualistic intuition pump is particularly weak in that it consists in setting up an evidently ridiculous straw man. That there is an intuition pump rather than an argument in the background here is revealed if one takes into account just how conceptually different Dennett's two definitions of dualism are. What is doing the work, the claim that there are not two kinds

of stuff or the claim that there is no stuff that is exempt from the laws of physical nature? Dennett presents a maximally simplified version of "dualism" and then rightly claims that it should be avoided, without pausing to make any respectable case to the effect that genuine dualists never even came close to his "dualism." To use one of his phrases against him: "This is a clear case of a misused intuition pump, where simplicity is doing all the work" (ibid.: 32). Another example of this tendency is Dennett's claim that Descartes adhered to the view of the mind "as an indivisible and perfectly self-communicating whole" (ibid.: 40). As usual in the genre of ascribing *n'importe quoi* to Descartes, Dennett does not provide a reference for this claim, and it is unlikely that he will find one, because Descartes did not hold the views Dennett calls "dualism" and "naïve perfectionism" respectively.

34 I will not even delve into the fact that the term "the brain" is equally problematic. For one thing, there is no single organ rightly called "the brain." Currently, no one has any idea how all the systems we group under "the nervous system" actually hang together, since these systems together turn out to be too complex for any actual scientifically respectable overall claim concerning "the brain." All of this is aggravated by the individuality of our nervous systems and their diachronic plasticity. The idea of "the human brain" happens to be an ideal type or construct regulating research and nothing out there in reality. Thanks to the neuroscientist Robert Nitsch for pointing this out to me and for showing me in detail how a good deal of the mind–brain problem in mainstream philosophy of mind is drawing on fantasies about the brain rather than on actual neuroscience. For Nitsch's philosophical views on this issue, see Nitsch (2012).

35 On this, see also Roger Scruton's recent defense of the basic approach to action explanation found in Kant, Fichte, and Hegel (Scruton 2017).

36 My version actually denies that there is such a thing as a largest possible ontological or epistemological frame. See Gabriel (2015a, 2015b).

37 For more on this, see Gabriel (2017: 98–9).

38 I have argued for this in detail in Gabriel (2014). An English translation of this is in preparation for Polity Press.

Chapter 4 Human Life and its Concept

1 See, for example, Hegel's critique of Kant in his early writing in Hegel (1988).

2 Kant (1902–), AA3, B 404 (my translation, with reference to the B-edition).
3 Ibid., AA3, B 72.
4 See Hegel (1976: Ch. 5).
5 This does not mean that there are no properties that are shared by all forms of life. Clearly there are such properties. For example, as a matter of empirical fact, DNA molecules play a crucial role in the reproduction of all terrestrial forms of life, both plants and animals. However, we can recognize that DNA plays this role in any given case only by comprehending what it does through a principle that places it in the activity that constitutes a certain life form. That this principle bears a different form in animals from the one it does in plants does not mean that it cannot make use of the same kind of molecule. Nothing can be comprehended as having a function in the reproduction of animal life other than in the context of a self-sustaining activity whose form is defined by sensory consciousness and, specifically, desire. This holds not only for reproduction and its organs (DNA is an organ of reproduction in the broad sense) but equally for digestion or perception. This needs to be articulated further (see, for example, the essays in Kern and Kietzmann (2017), including my "Kant über selbstbewusste Sinnlichkeit und die Idee menschlicher Entwicklung"). It is not my objective here to develop the Aristotelian account of formally distinct principles of life but to remind us of its existence and point out that it is immune to the dilemma to which, as I argue above, Gabriel falls victim.
6 The Aristotelian position does not deny that it is possible to apply mental concepts such as "knowledge" or "memory" to non-human animals. Consideration of so-called animal minds provides no refutation of the Aristotelian view. Rather, the view holds that the meaning of these concepts in application to animal life is different from the one that they have in application to human life. The generality that they nonetheless also possess is explained precisely by the sequence in which Aristotle places the different forms of life-principles.

Chapter 5 Replies

1 See Tononi and Koch (2015). I thank Giulio Tononi for intensive discussion of these issues during the Congreso Futuro organized by the Chilean government in January 2018. Fortunately, the Chilean senator Guido Girardi and his team thought that, intellectually, Giulio and I would enjoy traveling together through Chile (including a trip to Antarctica and Patagonia), which gave us some time to exchange thoughts on consciousness and mindedness. Two

other scientists have shaped my understanding of the brain part of the mind–brain problem: Armin Cremers, a brilliant computer scientist from my home institution, the University of Bonn, and Robert Nitsch, neuroscientist and director of the University of Münster's hospital. I thank them for destroying my illusion that we are entitled to assume that there is a unified organ within our skull that we successfully refer to with the word "the brain."

2 See recently Ellis (2016). For a helpful overview over the philosophical views and publications by Einstein, Schrödinger, Heisenberg, and others, see Scheibe (2012).

3 For more on this, see Gabriel (2017).

4 On the notion of freedom in my Neo-Existentialist framework, see ibid., Ch. 5.

5 This formal structure of humanity is not (yet) implemented institutionally despite the fact that ever since the dawn of modernity, and specifically ever since the French Revolution, there has been the hope among thinkers who embrace humanity that socio-political history tends towards a unification of all humans under the supreme formal norm of their capacity of self-constitution. It would lead too far afield to argue that we could derive positive socio-political content from our self-constitution, as this was not my intention in the work under discussion here.

6 This is a formulation of Charles Travis's from a book manuscript on Frege which he presented and discussed at a joint seminar at the International Centre for Philosophy at the University of Bonn in the summer semester 2017.

7 On one such story, see Assmann (2009, 1998).

8 To be subject to a norm, even if it is a rational norm (such as an inference pattern), need not involve consciousness of that fact on the part of the agent. See Burge (2013: 166ff.). Normativity, thus, is not sufficient for our grasp of our mindedness. Rather, specific forms of normativity, such as the activity of self-consciously aiming at the truth about our mindedness, exhibit the form that is required to draw a norm/nature distinction that does the job Benoist assigns to it. For the sake of the argument, I assume that the details of a relevant account of the specific normativity of the mental are filled in. In any event, some norms are natural kinds in my sense of the term, so that normativity cannot be the mark of the mental to the extent to which we distinguish it at all from the natural or physical.

9 On this, see the recent defense of a narrative ontology of the self in Hutter (2017).

10 This aspect of my ontology of fictional objects draws on Kablitz (2012). For more on this, see Gabriel (2016b).

11 This is how I read the cataphoric reference of "this fact" in Kern's text.

12 For an interesting non-reductionist account of the causal web correlated to consciousness, see Tononi and Koch (2015).

13 For an overview of the most recent development of non-mechanistic accounts of life in natural science, see Capra and Luisi (2017).

References

Assmann, J. (1998) *Moses the Egyptian: The Memory of Egypt in Western Monotheism*. Cambridge, MA: Harvard University Press.

Assmann, J. (2009) *The Prize of Monotheism*. Stanford, CA: Stanford University Press.

Azzouni, J. (2010) *Talking about Nothing: Numbers, Hallucinations, and Fictions*. New York: Oxford University Press.

Benoist, J. (2001) *Représentations sans objet: aux origines de la phénoménologie et de la philosophie analytique*. Paris: PUF.

Bishop, R. and Atmanspacher, A. (2011) The causal closure of physics and free will, in R. Kane (ed.), *Oxford Handbook of Free Will*. Oxford: Oxford University Press, pp. 101–11.

Blumenberg, H. (1985) *The Legitimacy of the Modern Age*. Cambridge, MA: MIT Press.

Brock, S. and Everett, A. (eds) (2015) *Fictional Objects*. Oxford: Oxford University Press.

Burge, T. (2013) *Cognition through Understanding: Self-Knowledge, Interlocution, Reasoning, Reflection, Philosophical Essays*, Vol. 3. Oxford: Oxford University Press.

Capra F. and Luisi, P. L. (2017) *The Systems View of Life: A Unifying Vision*. Cambridge: Cambridge University Press.

Cavell, S. (1999) *The Claim of Reason: Wittgenstein, Skepticism, Morality, and Tragedy*. Oxford: Oxford University Press.

Chakravartty, A. (2017) *Scientific Ontology: Integrating*

Naturalized Metaphysics and Voluntarist Epistemology.
Oxford: Oxford University Press.

Chalmers, D. (1996) *The Conscious Mind: In Search of a Fundamental Theory.* Oxford: Oxford University Press.

Chalmers, D. (2006a) The foundations of two-dimensional semantics, in M. García-Carpintero and J. Macià (eds), *Two-Dimensional Semantics: Foundations and Applications.* Oxford: Oxford University Press, pp. 55–140.

Chalmers, D. (2006b) Two-dimensional semantics, in E. Lepore and B. Smith (eds), *The Oxford Handbook of Philosophy of Language.* Oxford: Oxford University Press, pp. 575–606.

Chalmers, D. (2009) The two-dimensional argument against materialism, in B. P. McLaughlin, A. Beckermann and S. Walter (eds), *The Oxford Handbook of Philosophy of Mind.* Oxford: Oxford University Press, pp. 313–35.

Chang, H. (2012) *Is Water H_2O? Evidence, Realism and Pluralism.* Dordrecht: Springer.

Chomsky, N. (1975). *Reflections on Language.* New York: Pantheon Books.

Chomsky, N. (1988) *Language and Problems of Knowledge: The Managua Lectures.* Cambridge, MA: MIT Press.

Clark, A., and Chalmers, D. (1998) The extended mind, *Analysis*, 58(1): 7–19.

Dellian, E. (2007) *Die Rehabilitierung des Galileo Galilei oder die Kritik der Kantischen Vernunft.* Sankt Augustin: Academia.

Dennett, D. (1984) *Elbow Room: The Varieties of Free Will Worth Wanting.* Cambridge, MA: MIT Press.

Dennett, D. (1991) *Consciousness Explained.* Boston: Back Bay Books.

Dennett, D. (1992) The self as the center of narrative gravity, in F. S. Kessel, P. M. Cole, and D. L. Johnson (eds), *Self and Consciousness: Multiple Perspectives.* Mahwah, NJ: Lawrence Erlbaum, pp. 103–15.

Dennett, D. (2017) *From Bacteria to Bach and Back: The Evolution of Minds.* New York: W. W. Norton.

Ellis, G. F. R. (2016) *How Can Physics Underlie the Mind? Top-Down Causation in the Human Context.* Berlin: Springer.

Gabriel, M. (2014) *An den Grenzen der Erkenntnistheorie:*

Die notwendige Endlichkeit des objektiven Wissens als Lektion des Skeptizismus. 2nd edn, Freiburg: Karl Alber.

Gabriel, M. (2015a) *Fields of Sense: A New Realist Ontology.* Edinburgh: Edinburgh University Press.

Gabriel, M. (2015b) *Why the World Does Not Exist.* Cambridge: Polity.

Gabriel, M. (2016a) What kind of an idealist (if any) is Hegel?, *Hegel Bulletin*, 37(2): 181–208.

Gabriel, M. (2016b) Repliken auf Diehl/Rosefeldt, Hübner, Rödl und Stekeler-Weithofer, in T. Buchheim (ed.), *Jahrbuch-Kontroversen 2: Markus Gabriel: Neutraler Realismus.* Freiburg: Karl Alber, pp. 165–222.

Gabriel, M. (2017) *I am Not a Brain: Philosophy of Mind for the Twenty-First Century.* Cambridge: Polity.

Gabriel, M. and Žižek, S. (2009) *Mythology, Madness and Laughter: Subjectivity in German Idealism.* London: Continuum.

Görnitz, T. and Görnitz, B. (2016) *Von der Quantenphysik zum Bewusstsein: Kosmos, Geist und Materie.* Berlin: Springer.

Hegel, G. W. F. (1976) *The Phenomenology of Spirit*, trans. A. V. Miller. Oxford: Oxford University Press.

Hegel, G. W. F. (1988) *Faith and Knowledge*, ed. and trans. W. Cerf and H. S. Harris. New York: State University of New York Press.

Hegel, G. W. F. (2010) *Philosophy of Mind*, trans. W. Wallace and A. V. Miller, rev. M. Inwood. Oxford: Oxford University Press.

Henrich, D. (2007) *Denken und Selbstsein: Vorlesungen über Subjektivität.* Berlin: Suhrkamp.

Hofweber, T. (2016) *Ontology and the Ambitions of Metaphysics.* Oxford: Oxford University Press.

Husserl, E. (1970) *The Crisis of European Sciences and Transcendental Phenomenology.* Evanston, IL: Northwestern University Press.

Hutter, A. (2017) *Narrative Ontologie.* Tübingen: Mohr Siebeck.

Jackson, F. (1986) What Mary didn't know, *Journal of Philosophy*, 83(5): 291–5.

Jackson, F. (1998) *From Metaphysics to Ethics: A Defense of a Conceptual Analysis.* Oxford: Clarendon Press.

120 References

Kablitz, A. (2012) *Kunst des Möglichen: Theorie der Literatur*. Freiburg im Breisgau: Rombach.

Kant, I. (1902–). *Kants gesammelte Schriften*, ed. Deutschen (Königlich Preußischen) Akademie der Wissenschaften, 29 vols. Berlin: Walter de Gruyter.

Kant, I. (1992) Dreams of a spirit seer elucidated by dreams of metaphysics, in *Immanuel Kant: Theoretical philosophy, 1755–1770*, ed. and trans. D. Walford. Cambridge: Cambridge University Press, pp. 301–59.

Kant, I. (2015) *Critique of Practical Reason*, ed. and trans. M. Gregor. Cambridge: Cambridge University Press.

Kern, A., and Kietzmann, C. (eds) (2017) *Selbstbewusstes Leben: Texte zu einer transformativen Theorie der menschlichen Subjektivität*. Berlin: Suhrkamp.

Levine, J. (2004) *Purple Haze: The Puzzle of Consciousness*. Oxford: Oxford University Press.

Lewens, T. (2015) *Cultural Evolution: Conceptual Challenges*. Oxford: Oxford University Press.

McGinn, C. (1993) *The Problem of Consciousness: Essays Towards Resolution*. New York: Wiley.

McGinn, C. (1999) *The Mysterious Flame: Conscious Minds in a Material World*. New York: Basic Books.

Nagel, T. (1989) *The View from Nowhere*. Oxford: Oxford University Press.

Nagel, T. (2012) *Mind and Cosmos: Why the Materialist Neo-Darwinian Conception of Nature is Almost Certainly False*. Oxford: Oxford University Press.

Nitsch, R. (2012) *Gehirn, Geist und Bedeutung: Zur Stellung der Neurowissenschaften in der Leib-Seele-Diskussion*. Münster: Mentis.

Noë, A. (2009) *Out of Our Heads: Why You Are Not Your Brain, and Other Lessons from the Biology of Consciousness*. New York: Hill & Wang.

Pinker, S. (1997) *How the Mind Works*. New York: W. W. Norton.

Popper, K., and Eccles, J. (1977) *The Self and its Brain: An Argument for Interactionism*. Berlin: Springer.

Price, H. (2011) *Naturalism without Mirrors*. Oxford: Oxford University Press.

Putnam, H. (1981) *Reason, Truth, and History*. Cambridge: Cambridge University Press.

Putnam, H. (1992) *Realism with a Human Face*. Cambridge, MA: Harvard University Press.

Putnam, H. (2012) *Philosophy in an Age of Science: Physics, Mathematics, and Skepticism*. Cambridge, MA: Harvard University Press.

Quine, W. V. O. (1960) *Word and Object*. Cambridge, MA: MIT Press.

Rayo, A. (2013) *The Construction of Logical Space*. Oxford: Oxford University Press.

Ricoeur, P. (1992) *Oneself as Another*. Chicago: University of Chicago Press.

Robinson, H. (2017) Dualism, in E. Zalta (ed.), *The Stanford Encyclopedia of Philosophy*, https://plato.stanford.edu/archives/fall2017/entries/dualism/.

Scheibe, E. (2012) *Die Philosophie der Physiker*. Munich: Beck.

Schelling, F. W. J. (2014) *Zeitschrift für spekulative Physik*, Vol. 2. Hamburg: Meiner.

Schelling, F. W. J. (2017) *Zeitschrift für spekulative Physik*, Vol. 1. Hamburg: Meiner.

Scruton, R. (2017) *On Human Nature*. Princeton, NJ: Princeton University Press.

Searle, J. (2010) *Making the Social World: The Structure of Human Civilization*. New York: Oxford University Press.

Sellars, W. (1963) *Science, Perception and Reality*. London: Routledge & Kegan Paul.

Shear, J. (1997) *Explaining Consciousness: The "Hard Problem"*. Cambridge, MA: MIT Press.

Tallis, R. (2014) *Aping Mankind: Neuromania, Darwinitis and the Misrepresentation of Humanity*. London: Routledge.

Taylor, C. (1964) *The Explanation of Behaviour*. London: Routledge & Kegan Paul.

Taylor, C. (1985a) *Philosophical Papers*, Vol. 1: *Human Agency and Language*. Cambridge: Cambridge University Press.

Taylor, C. (1985b) *Philosophical Papers*, Vol. 2: *Philosophy and the Human Sciences*. Cambridge: Cambridge University Press.

Taylor, C. (2007) *A Secular Age*. Cambridge, MA: Harvard University Press.

Tetens, H. (2015) *Gott denken: Ein Versuch über rationale Theologie*. Stuttgart: Reclam.

Tononi, G. and Koch, C. (2015) Consciousness: here, there, and everywhere?, *Philosophical Transactions of the Royal Society B*, 370: 20140167.

Varela, F., Thompson, E., and Rosch, E. (2016 [1991]). *The Embodied Mind: Cognitive Science and Human Experience*. Cambridge, MA: MIT Press.

Index